MARY'S
MESSAGE
OF
LOVE

MARY'S MESSAGE OF LOVE

AS SENT BY MARY,
THE MOTHER OF JESUS,
TO HER MESSENGER

ANNIE KIRKWOOD

BLUE DOLPHIN

Published by Blue Dolphin Publishing, Inc.
P.O. Box 8, Nevada City, CA 95959
Orders: 1-800-643-0765
Web page: http://www.bluedolphinpublishing.com

ISBN: 0-931892-33-3

Library of Congress Cataloging-in-Publication Data

Mary, Blessed Virgin, Saint (Spirit)
    Mary's message of love : as sent by Mary, the mother of Jesus, to her
messenger / [received by] Annie Kirkwood.
        p.   cm.
    Includes bibliographical references (p.   ).
    ISBN 0-931892-33-3 (alk. paper)
    1. Spirit writings.   2. Spiritual life.   I. Kirkwood, Annie,
1937–   .   II. Title.
    BF1301M365 1999
    133.9'3—dc21   99-41935
                                                            CIP

Cover painting by Tamara Berault

First printing, August, 1999
Second edition, January, 2001

Printed in the United States of America

10   9   8   7   6   5   4   3   2

Table of Contents

Introduction

THIS BOOK IS UNUSUAL because, while the emphasis is on Mother Mary's new messages, Mother Mary has asked me to include the information I use in the workshops entitled, "Love—A Healing Energy" and "Forgiveness." I didn't know how to write it down, or feel it was something I could do. Of course, I told Mother Mary this. She is so very loving and gentle that, when she doesn't want to enter into a discussion about one of her requests, she will simply restate her request. It seemed that this was important information that she wanted included in this book, so I've done my best to include the basic information.

There is much that goes on in any workshop or seminar. Over the years, I've noticed that, even if I'm using the same information, each workshop will be entirely different than the last. Group dynamics, and where people have questions or thoughts to share, will at times take the workshop into new, untried areas.

During each workshop, I tell many examples of how I've used the material in Mother Mary's messages to change my life. It's one thing to expose my vulnerabilities and frailties to people who I can see, but quite another to see them in print!

Also, when I am there in person, I can often clear up some misconceptions of what I said. Being present in a group allows me to feel safe and comfortable about revealing so much about myself. The most difficult part of Mother Mary's request has been to include the Love/Forgiveness workshop. I'm going on trust that, when you read my part, you will remember that I am only using myself as an example in hopes that it will spark something in you to use all of Mother Mary's messages to improve your life.

All of my adult life my major concern has been for my children. Somewhere along the way I was taught that family was important. I'm not sure how, or where, or who taught me this, but it seems to be a part of my general make-up. In 1988 I defined family as those people who were related to me by blood, marriage, or a deep friendship. Today I've learned to expand that concept to include not only the above description, but all people in general. Mother Mary has taught me to love all people, and to consider them a part of my family, the family of humanity. She has taught me to love not only my family, but to love all people, as they too are children of God. I don't always like my human family, neither do I always agree, or condone their actions, but loving them is my way of showing God how much I love His creation.

Many of Mother Mary's lessons have to do with love. My favorite chapter in *Mary's Message to the World* is the chapter on Love. Through Her, I'm learning to love unconditionally. This way of loving has made a tremendous improvement in my life, my marriage, and my relationship with my children. Also, it has made a tremendous improvement in my self-esteem, as I learn to love myself unconditionally. Occasionally I slip and find myself berating or chastising myself over something I said or did. But most of the time I forgive myself and remind myself that I now love unconditionally, and that is how God loves us all the time.

It really is quite freeing to love unconditionally. It means that no longer must I figure out why someone has acted, or not acted, in a certain way. I used to think that if I could understand what a person's reason was for what they did, I could accept and love them. Now I don't need to understand, all I need to do is accept them, just as they are, without judging. It's what we all seek—to be accepted for who we are. So I feel that in reality I'm living up to Jesus' golden rule, to "do unto others as I would have them do unto me."

My grandchildren really, really know that no matter what they do, say, or think, I love them. I don't always condone or agree with their decisions or behaviors, but I love them. My adult children have expressed their gratitude for my love and say it's been a big help to them to know that I am there for them, loving them no matter what. My husband really appreciates my unconditional love. He remembers what it was like when I loved conditionally. Today he feels truly loved because no matter what . . . I love him. My stepchildren have repeatedly told me they love me and that they appreciate the love we share. All of us are a complete family unit. There isn't the old feeling of these are Byron's children, or these are mine.* I've watched them introduce friends to their stepbrothers, and it is done with pride and love. You can hear it in their voices. Our sons greet each other with a hug and genuine love. One Mother's Day, I received a card from one of my stepsons that read as follows: "You're a great step-mom . . . (turn the page) . . . Thank God you didn't read Cinderella!" My first reaction was, "Of course

---

*We are a blended family.

I've read Cinderella." It took a while for the verse to have meaning. I don't act like Cinderella's step-mom to them. But most importantly, I've stopped acting like Cinderella's step-mother to myself. Loving unconditionally has brought our family together in a bond that is very strong and very healthy. Not only have I learned to love unconditionally, but so have my husband and our children.

From the point of being the recipient of unconditional love, I can tell you it's a most wonderful and secure feeling. It allows you to be yourself at all times, without fear of being censored. It's the freedom to express your viewpoint, even if it isn't what the rest of the family thinks, feels, or believes. It's the security that you are safe and accepted at all times, the assurance that your welfare is considered. Nothing else can feel so good, not even romantic love. Nothing else is so healing. Nothing else gives you the security to be totally honest with yourself. Nothing else can bond a family together so gently, yet allow each member to express, behave, and be who they are in the depth of their heart.

Included in this book is the material I use in the workshop titled, "Love—A Healing Energy," and in the newer "Forgiveness" workshop. Most of the material used in the workshops has been given to me as the books were, through inner messages that I type on my computer. But much of it comes from personal experiences, as I've done my best to **"Live the message"** as Mother Mary instructed me to do. Some of the material draws from other sources that I've used, and I will tell you about these sources as we go along. Included are exercises, suggestions, and ideas I use to heal and keep my heart clear of anger and fear, and to live in unconditional love. I'll also answer some of the more frequently asked questions.

I hope these comments, insights, and suggestions help you find the love that is deep within your heart. It's the love which comes from "the Father within" as Jesus referred to God, and it's the "Kingdom of Heaven" that he said is within each of us. God's unconditional love truly is a healing and powerful energy. My prayer is that you, too, if you don't already, experience the joy of loving unconditionally.

Annie Kirkwood

PART 1

*Unconditional Love
and Forgiveness*

1

Love—A Healing Energy

THIS IS THE TITLE OF A WORKSHOP that I've been giving across the country since 1993. It's difficult to have the flavor and feeling of a workshop in print, because much is dependent on the active participation of the people attending. But there is a lot of good information that could be useful to you as you incorporate unconditional love into your daily life. During a workshop we enjoy group meditations and other experiential exercises that bring home our capability to feel the energy of love. I answer questions, share from my own experiences the ways I've used the material presented, and I encourage the participants to share. In no way does this mean that I think I have the correct, or right way, of using the information. So please remember, this is a sharing of myself, not to say "I know the way," but to let you know that I am human, experiencing very real fears, and very justified angers. In sharing I am encouraging you to find the way to live in love and peace.

As I began to hold workshops, one of my fears had been that I don't have a traditional educational background, which I thought was needed to give a workshop: you know, those two- or three-letter initials you often see behind some people's names to indicate they have years of education and study.

When I talked this over with Mary, She said I was to draw from my storehouse of personal experiences. I was to share the ways I've used the material and what I've learned from working with it. She told me I was to urge, encourage, and support people as they begin to live Her message.

Appearing in public has not been easy to do. When I first began to give talks and hold workshops, often I talked as tears spilled out of my eyes. It was very painful to bare my soul. People could easily see how difficult it was. What happened was that others would open up their hearts and could share some of their experiences. Many said they had similar experiences and couldn't believe that I could ever love myself or forgive my abusers.* Thus the workshops took on the flavor and feel of the people who were attending. So I encourage you to find the way to live in unconditional love and to do it as best as you can.

Think for a moment, as you concentrate on love, UN-CONDITIONAL LOVE, for any given time period—notice how uplifted and inspired you feel. Unconditional love, as we humans experience it, is the closest love on earth to Divine Love. We need love in our lives in order to survive, just as we need water and food. It's essential to our well-being, our human existence, and to mankind's survival.

_____

*This refers to my childhood sexual abuse.

Most people already know about the benefits of touch and attention to newborn babies and its importance to their growth. This was blatantly demonstrated to the world when the orphanages of Romania became the topic of interest on national TV a few years ago. The children in these orphanages were below their normal weight, considered somewhat retarded in mental and emotional development, and appeared listless and uninterested in their surroundings. Their hair and eyes were dull. It seemed that the light of life in their eyes was dim. Left in their cribs without personal attention or affection, they languished. The attention they received was nominal because there were so few workers to feed them or keep them dry and moderately clean.

For years the general public has had the knowledge that plants grow more profusely if given attention (love). In recent years, there have been many studies on geriatric patients in nursing homes. They, too, show that a lack of attention is one of the reasons for the patients' decline in physical and mental health.

All these types of studies point out that love is a necessity, like air, food, water, and shelter. We need attention and love so that we can grow and progress in life. We need acceptance and appreciation and all the different aspects of love in our daily life. When we don't receive the right kind of love, or we don't get enough love, especially as children, we develop problems. Often I'm questioned about my use of the term "the right kind of love." What I'm talking about, in separating love into right kind and other types, is unconditional love and conditional love. Many people grow up knowing only conditional or judgmental love. The kind of love that says, "I will love you, or love you more . . . if you, when you, or after you do something." The request may be legal or illegal, necessary or unnecessary, nice or at times cruel. If you have to do some deed, or behave in some way that is not your usual way, or you must curtail or diminish yourself in order to be loved . . . there is no doubt it is conditional love.

The love that heals is unconditional love. This is the love that says "I love you" no matter what happens, or what you do or don't do. It's the love we all seek. It's the love that soothes the soul, calms the anxious heart, and brings peace into troubled lives. I will talk about unconditional love later; there are many misconceptions, and these will be discussed.

I realize that I used to spend more time loving conditionally and only loved certain people unconditionally in specific circumstances. I have a son, Mark, with Down's Syndrome, and it's the only way I love him. There were never any expectations or standards with this child. We were told he was severely retarded and not to expect him to be able to sit up, much less take care of himself. With each of his accomplishments we rejoiced. Mark went beyond our expectation for him. My other children came after Mark, and although I tried to love them unconditionally, it was easy to let my expectations for them cloud my love. It wasn't until they were older that I realized I could still love them as I did Mark yet not like their particular behavior.

More than once I was told that Mark progressed beyond his expected area of activity because we loved him. He was not expected to live beyond a few days, and he is now 41 years old (in 1997). One doctor said to me, when Mark was very ill with pneumonia, "Let him go, you are holding him here." My belief was that I loved Mark and wanted him to live, but when God was ready for him, Mark would die and nothing I did, or didn't do, would stop it. Unconditional love not only gives us peace, but it frees us to be our best, to go beyond all our expectations.

During the time I was receiving the message that became the book, *Mary's Message to the World,* Mother Mary said, "The first step to being prepared is to learn to love yourself." At the time when I heard the words "being prepared," I was thinking of the terrible storms, earthquakes, and what is now generally called "Earth changes." My preconceived ideas about how to be prepared were strictly physical. I expected Mary to tell me to "move," then give me the name of the road in Montana, the name of a real estate agent, and a grocery list. You know, 500 pounds of beans and rice (you can tell I'm Mexican-American), water, and other food staples. So to be told to love myself was very confusing.

I asked Her, "How is this going to help?" There was no answer. Often I don't receive an answer directly. It is better for me to figure it out for myself, because it's clearer and takes root in my consciousness. When I first began to work with Mother Mary and asked questions for which I didn't receive an answer, I became not only confused, but felt more anxious and afraid that perhaps I hadn't heard the answer. What I've found is that when I don't get an answer, if I ask a different question, I may receive an answer that gives a clearer understanding. So at times it seems that I need to ask the "right" question in order to get an answer. A few days later, as I thought about learning to love myself as the first step, I then asked, "How am I supposed to do that?" The immediate answer was, "As best you can." I said to Mary, "Gee, that's a lot of help!" Again, I heard, "Do it as best you can." The presence and perception of the voice has always been very loving and very patient.

Since then, I've spent years working diligently to learn to love myself. All we can ever do is our best, or "as best we can." It's been a great source of comfort to know that nothing more

is expected of me, that what is expected of me is something I
am capable of. There have been times when I will judge
myself and find I haven't been complying very well with
Mother Mary's request that I learn to love myself. It has
taken years to see that when my intention is to do my best,
that is what I will do. If I set up some predetermined goal to
indicate my best, then I could very well be disappointed. But
if, daily, I get up with the prayer of doing my best that day
and to truly live one day at a time, then I am successful. So
. . . yesterday I could set the world on fire and performed like
a well-oiled machine. If today I can barely move and my
mind is mush, all that is expected is that I do my best today.
It doesn't mean that I must perform as I did the day before.
Each day is judged separately and apart from any other day.
This is why the knowledge, that all that's required is our best,
is such a great comfort. This gives me confidence in my
ability to do my best, and it motivates me to continue to do
my best.

When Mother Mary said I was to learn to love myself, I
lived in great fear with an undiagnosed case of agoraphobia,
meaning that, because of fear, I couldn't leave my home
alone. When I did, I suffered severe panic attacks. This
condition began slowly and insidiously. There were times I
functioned like everyone else. I could go to the grocery store
alone, or to a mall. Later, I began to notice that I became
uncomfortable and antsy. But I could get out of the house if
I wasn't gone too long. Later I realized that it was best for me
to meet someone. Over the years it became more and more
difficult to leave my house for any reason. Then it became
difficult to leave my house in the company of another person.
When Mary first began to visit me, I had trouble leaving my
house even with my husband, whom I trusted above all

others. There were places I could not go, no matter who was with me, or how many people were with me. During the last year that I worked as a nurse, before Mary first visited me, for some unknown reason I could go to work without much discomfort. Sometimes when my shift was over, the urge to get into my house was very strong. I trembled inside until I walked into my home.

There were periods of time when the symptoms would almost go away. During the regression of symptoms, I would feel that I'd dreamed the panic. But then it would return, at times more severe, and at other times only mildly symptomatic. I made all kinds of excuses: "I didn't like to go anywhere by myself. . . . I wasn't used to being alone (I had taken my children and neighborhood children with me most of my early adult life). . . . I had more fun when I was with another person." Finally I said to family and friends who urged me to overcome this inability, "I just don't want to go alone!" However the truth was that I lived in terror, and wouldn't, or couldn't admit it to myself.

I think now that I was in so much denial because, if I admitted it, then I had a large problem and it would require a solution, or treatment. I was in complete denial of how severe and how incapacitating the problem was. I admitted I had a lot of fears. As I received the message, Mother Mary's call to "cleanse your heart of fear and anger," it was a personal call to me. So I began the process of trying to live Mary's message, AND . . . **the first step was to learn to love myself.**

What was love anyway? I asked myself. Maybe I didn't really know what love was, so I looked it up in the dictionary. The first definition in *The American College Dictionary* is "a strong or passionate affection for a person of the opposite sex." But is this all there is to love? Did this definition give an accurate description of love? What about a mother's love, or the love for a pet, or what about loving a friend, no matter the gender and without any sexual overtones. My question was, "Is sex so tied to love in our culture that we cannot think of one without the other?" No wonder our society has trouble with love. The seventh definition in the dictionary was, "The benevolent affection of God for His creatures." When I read this, I was amazed that God's love would rank last in *The American College Dictionary.*

Myths

It is my opinion that our society really doesn't understand the subject of love. There are countless songs, poems, and stories written about love. We talk about love, sing about love, portray love in movies, but not many of us live from a heart filled with unconditional love. Most of the stories and songs are of the "someone-did-me-wrong" type. We either think of love in a lofty, poetic way . . . or we think of love as lusty or abusive. We've created many misconceptions and ideas about love. Soon after I'd begun to give this workshop, I attended a workshop given by a couple of my friends on Prosperity and Abundance.* They discussed the myths surrounding money. This led me to think about myths in general. Once again I went to the dictionary and looked up the word "myth" and all the myth-based words. The first definition is, "A traditional or legendary story, usually concerning some superhuman being or some alleged person or event, whether without or with a determinable basis of fact or

---

*"Prosperity and Abundance Workshop" facilitated by Anita Marcos and Connie Cornwell of Dallas, Texas.

a natural explanation." The fifth definition of the word "mythical" is, "having no foundation in fact: imaginary; fictitious."

Myths, then, are traditional or legendary stories. In our society and culture we have many traditional and legendary stories based on love that have created untold misconceptions of love. As an example, think about Shakespeare's *Romeo and Juliet,* the ultimate story of young love. I wonder how many youngsters have ended their lives when parents tried to stop them from seeing each other, believing suicide is the ultimate act of love. But the story that stands out in my mind is the movie, *Love Story.* I think this movie script did more to confuse our concept of love than we are aware of. The famous line of that story is, "Love is never having to say you're sorry." My response is, "If you love me, you'd better be able to say you're sorry!" One day a friend visited me after he'd had an argument with his wife. He needed to talk, and I was willing to listen. But after listening to him for a while, I asked him what he thought love was. He responded with, "Love is never having to say you're sorry." I asked, "Even when you've wronged your mate, you think you can't, or shouldn't, say you're sorry?" I'm not sure that my comments helped him to understand what I was getting at. Sometimes what people need is to be listened to, so they can hear their own thoughts as they are verbalized into words.

I honestly believe the writer of this movie was implying that, if we love wholeheartedly, we will never knowingly cause our loved ones pain, or upset them in any way. Therefore, according to that way of thinking, there will never be a need to say you're sorry. But let's face it . . . we are all human. We can't read each other's minds, nor are we always in tune with our loved ones on an emotional and mental level. I've seen how my flip and off-handed remarks can hurt my husband, if he isn't in the mood to be teased. At times I take Byron's teasing, and half-teasing comments with grace and a good laugh. But at other times, the same words will cause me to flare up in outrage, and I take his comments as a personal insult. It's inconceivable to me that anyone would think that a person could always be so in sync with their loved ones, that they would immediately know when there was a mood change and what that mood really is.

Our personal history affects the way we think and feel about things, not to mention all the other things, like family dynamics, family myths, family beliefs, neighborhood or cultural ideas and standards. I don't know all the past situations and occurrences that happened to, and around, Byron. I'm sure there were situations that caused him to be embarrassed or disappointed as a child, which affect him today. Most people have these types of situations that occurred in their childhood. In my own experience, the childhood sexual abuse that I lived through affects me even today. After years of therapy and my own commitment to healing, there are times when a memory can affect how I feel. Perhaps on a particular day I don't feel like being teased. I need to state that it's been a blessing that my father was not one of my abusers; however, other family members were. I've been told that, because my father was a good role model, I've had an easier time in healing than many who were betrayed by an abusing father.

Incest isn't the only abuse that hurts people. Many people have suffered other types of childhood abuse. Many come from homes where one or both parents drank or were emotionally or mentally distraught, or ill. Many suffer from abandonment and neglect. There are all kinds of ways a child can be affected. There is not only abuse but emotional, mental, and psychological needs that were not, or could not, be met. Perhaps you didn't suffer any abuse, but many people will have had some disappointment or embarrassment in their past, some way their family, peers, or teachers let them down or caused them untold pain. Children are often the cruelest to other children, and these memories can have an effect in adulthood. A parent's illness or death confuses, bewilders, and at times scars children. These types of childhood experiences affect us today and how we look at life and how we deal with life. To think that a person could go through life without having an occasion to say, "I'm sorry," isn't real in my opinion. We are all human, we all make mistakes, we all inadvertently say something at some time in our life that causes hurt feelings to those who are closest to us. So the idea that, "Love is never having to say you're sorry," is not founded on fact . . . it's a myth.

There are other myths that our culture has created. Many of us have our own set of myths that have been created from misconceptions, movies, and/or our misunderstanding of religious principles. Recently psychologists and mental health workers have been promoting the merits of self-esteem, and I see this as a vast improvement over the years when no one thought about self-esteem. We have created many myths about the topic of loving oneself. Remember that Mother Mary said, "The first step to being prepared is learning to love yourself." She also said that we are to love ourself, then our loved ones, and then the world. In other words, we begin with number one, ourselves. I've found that when I love myself unconditionally, it so much easier to be open and loving to others.

The following are some of my personal myths on self-love. Loving myself, I thought, was egotistical, self-centered, and narcissistic. I thought loving myself was the epitome of selfishness and self-centeredness. As we talked about myths in workshops, many of the people attending said they felt the same way. It seems many of us were taught to believe that it's a "no-no" to love oneself. I equated loving myself with being a bad person. I now feel that when we learn to love ourself first, we are more confident and free to love others, because our basic need for love is being met.

There are many more myths about love between men and women. Some of my own myths were: platonic friendships between men and women didn't exist . . . when men and women were together, there was always an underlying element of sexuality . . . men always want sex from women and that was all they thought about. During the angry "let's bash men" time of my life, I had many colorful ways to express this idea. Back to my personal myths . . . men use women for their own purposes, and occasionally there were some women who use men. You can tell how my history of sexual abuse formed many of my personal myths and much of what I believed to be true. Many people today believe that love and sex are synonymous.

There are just as many myths concerning unconditional love. Many people truly believe that never having to say you're sorry is what unconditional love is all about. I thought it meant becoming a doormat and allowing your loved ones to use you as you smiled sweetly. That when you love unconditionally, you endure everything and anything the person you love says and does. I thought loving unconditionally was smiling tenderly and quietly through your pain, never allowing anyone to know how difficult it was and always being agreeable, never saying no. Was I off-base on this subject or was I off-base? You can see how these myths kept me, and can keep you, from enjoying the benefits of unconditional love. My personal myths interfered with my ability to love myself and to freely love others.

So how did I change? How did I free myself from the myths that ruled my life for so many years? Awareness does much to change our consciousness. Becoming aware of a problem is the first step to change. When I became aware of the role myths play in our lives, it brought a new awareness. It gave me food for thought . . . something to mull over. In the beginning I thought about my myths when I did my housework and when I was quiet. Before attending a workshop on Abundance and Prosperity, I hadn't thought about the myths that have been created about money, and our ability to enjoy money and be spiritual. Before that day I'd only thought about myths as something we studied in high school about ancient times. But the idea that we create myths in our lives today, and that there are myths which are created by our culture, heritage, and religious beliefs, was a new and startling idea. In the workshop, we talked about how our culture has affected us and how these beliefs are handed down from generation to generation. This doesn't mean that families sit by the fireside and listen to stories about their myths, but children learn as if through osmosis from their parents, grandparents, and extended family. My inner guidance repeatedly says, "The best teacher is example." By the way people around us live their lives, their basic beliefs, and their basic values . . . we are taught.

I did an inner search to see what myths I had about loving myself, and later about loving unconditionally. I spent a lot of time in prayer and meditation. I prayed to be honest with myself, and to have all my erroneous, myth-based beliefs about loving myself revealed to me clearly. My inner longing

was to be free of the fear which was dominating my life. I was
sick and tired of being sick and tired, and scared. I couldn't
go anywhere without being uncomfortable at best, and at
worst experiencing panic attacks. If the only way for me to rid
myself of the debilitating fear was to learn to love myself,
then I resolved that is what I would do. It took decision,
commitment, and a desire to change. Without these three, I
don't think I would have really been able to make any
changes.

Learning to Love Yourself

It took a lot of prayer, a lot of meditation and thinking to
help me begin to see how wrong I had been in many of my
beliefs. It took even more prayer and courage to change an
erroneous belief system that had been in place for many years.
I began with **step one . . . learning to love yourself.** My first
misconception was that to love myself was an act of selfishness or self-centeredness. It was something distasteful, not
something I wanted to do. After much thought, I concluded
that selfishness and self-centeredness are not acts of a loving
person, but were acts of fearful people who are afraid they will
not get their fair share of love. At the time I couldn't see the
benefits of loving myself. If someone asked me, "Do you love
yourself?" I would indignantly answer, "NO!"

I went through life erroneously putting other people's
needs, or what I thought were their needs, first. I thought this
was being "Christian, good, and unselfish." Now I know that
I was really a raging co-dependent. I projected all of my fears
and angers on other people and then erroneously believed
that I could control their lives. It was easier to see how other

people should be living their lives, than to see what I was doing. I was good at telling people what they should be doing, eating, thinking, and what their decisions should be. This is an understatement; actually I was more than good at directing other people's lives. At the same time, I couldn't make a decision, didn't know what I was doing, didn't think about what I was eating, and certainly didn't put much thought into myself. I laughed a lot and was always making jokes, putting myself down, thinking this was being funny. I was not honest with myself and hid the many ways I sabotaged my life and those who could or would love me. If I thought someone didn't like me, or had become angry with me, I was instantly angry with them. I refused to talk to them, not giving them a chance to defend or explain what had happened. My myth was, "If I'm angry first, then it won't hurt as much." I left friendships, relationships, and marriages thinking that, if I left first, it wouldn't hurt as much. I wore my feelings on my sleeve, and my favorite expression was, "You hurt my feelings."

How did I change and learn to love myself? It wasn't easy, and it didn't happen overnight. But with persistence and determination, it can be accomplished. Among other things, I used affirmations, visualizations, self-guided meditations, and a modified version of Mother Mary's words as an affirmation: "**The first step is to learn to love myself, as best I can.**" I was already praying about this and had made the decision, and the commitment, and I had the desire to change my self-esteem. I recalled that Mother Mary said, "**God loves you more than you know, and He loves you just as you are.**" She said that nothing we do, say, think, or believe keeps God from loving us. So I used Mother Mary's words as my first affirmation: "**God loves me just as I am.**" I had gained a lot of weight during that year and was very self-conscious about it. What bothered me the most was my weight. I would wash dishes and vacuum the floor repeating over and over, "God loves me just as I am; even if I'm fat, God loves me." At the time I was not only fearful but angry.

Another affirmation was, "God loves me even if I'm afraid." "God loves me when I'm angry." Another affirmation I used was, "God loves me even if I'm so afraid I can't go to the grocery store." This was one of our bones of contention. Byron thought I should be able to go to the grocery store while he was at work, and I agreed it was logical. But I was too afraid of having a panic attack to comply and waited until he could go with me. One of the things I realized was that, in order to get over my fears, I had to face them. It was very scary, and just the thought left me trembling and nauseous. I thought of President Franklin Roosevelt, who said, "We have nothing to fear but fear itself." I thought about this statement a lot. I didn't exactly know how to use this information, yet I was determined to overcome my fears.

The most obvious fear was the fear of leaving my house. The incident that really demonstrated the extent of this fear was the morning Byron didn't bring in the newspaper from the front yard before he left for work. I had to go to the bedroom, which was over the garage, to see our front yard and, sure enough, there was the newspaper I had been looking for. I was so angry that I called Byron at work and said most indignantly, "You didn't bring in the paper this morning!" His nice, calm reply was, "You're right; if you want the paper, Annie, you will have to go outside and pick it up. You're afraid to do that?" I let him know I wasn't afraid; it was just very inconsiderate of him not to bring in the paper. Of course I could go outside. I wasn't that incapacitated, was I?

I ran out the front door, and by the time I reached the paper, I had broken out in a sweat, was trembling, nauseous, and my heart was racing. When I entered the house that day, there was no denying that I had a big problem. I could do several things to overcome it; the most reasonable was to seek professional help. But still, I felt that maybe I could handle it. After talking my situation over with Byron, I promised to do all I could to go out of the house without help. In the mornings I opened the garage door and stood at the doorway from the house to the garage. Then I began to step into the garage and away from the doorway. As I stood still, there was a lot of self-talk going on in my head. I used affirmations, encouragement, and anything I could think of to help me get past the fear I was feeling. Finally, after weeks, I was able to reach the end of the garage and stand in the doorway to the outside. I stayed at this point for several weeks. During this time, Byron called from work to encourage me to step outside. I would hang on to the cordless phone for dear life and stand at the patio door and look out at the pond below our deck. After several months I could go stand on the deck. It was a long, hard road to freedom from this fear, and these were only the beginning steps.

So when people say to me, "I'm so afraid," I fully understand their fear. I was enslaved by fear for many years. People who knew me before I isolated myself in my home will not believe that I was this afraid, because I covered my fear with bluster, anger, loud-talking, and laughing. But believe me, I do know what fear is, and it doesn't feel good. I encourage you to do whatever you can to be free of fear.

Mother Mary asked me to share my story and methods of healing. She said I was to be a support for people and their encourager. My role in life seems to be one of sharing my experiences. Letting people (strangers) know you, as if they were your friends, isn't easy. At times I feel I have no life, but then I get back in focus with my inner self and remember that I truly do have a life. It's a very human life, one in which I get to experience all the emotions, and often experience them to the extreme. I've known great fear and even greater love, overwhelming sadness and awesome joy, extreme anger and wonderful serenity. I have experienced all kinds of situations in my life. I've wished for death more than once, yet I am overjoyed to be living today. My friend, Marty, once said to me that I was afraid to die and I was afraid to live. This used to be true of me, but it's no longer true.

In the beginning, I used visualization exercises to help me learn to put the anger and fear outside of me. I bought a book titled *Healing Visualizations* by Gerald Epstein, M.D. (1989) which is filled with visualizations Dr. Epstein used in his medical practice with good results. In the last chapters he tells the readers how to create their own visualizations. I modified some of his visualizations and created new ones. Dr. Epstein also relates what his studies revealed about the many practical uses of visualization. I highly recommend this book, not only for physical ailments but for ailments of the heart. He says it takes 21 days to break an old habit and learn a new one. With emotional issues it sometimes takes longer, as it did for me.

One of his visualizations was for heart trouble, so I modified it to use for my kind of heart trouble—fear and anger. This visualization takes you to a fountain where golden brushes are used to clean out the heart. In a visualization, all is possible, and you will have whatever you need at hand, without thinking about it. In visualizations things happen without thought; whatever you need appears or disappears instantly. I imagined water that turns different colors, golden brushes that magically appear in my hand, and zippers that allowed me to remove my heart and open it without any problem. In my modified visualization, I unzip my chest, pull out my heart, and unzip the small zipper on my heart to cleanse the inside, without trying to use my logical mind to make sense of the process.

To do a visualization, first state your intention or reason for doing the visualization. Count your "out" breaths—not your inhalations but your exhalations. Breathe normally and let the air out through your mouth, relaxing as you do. By breathing in this fashion you bring about a light meditative mode. It isn't necessary to be in a deep meditative state of mind for visualization to work.

When I use visualization, I first state my intention—to rid my emotional self, my heart, of fear and anger . . . then I take three out-breaths. I find myself at a beautiful fountain. I can see my chest through my clothes; there is a zipper in the middle of my chest. I unzip my chest without having to open my clothes or take them off. There is no pain or discomfort. . . . I put my hand in my chest and pull out my heart. . . . In my hand appears a golden brush, one much like the scrubbing bubble brush on the TV commercial. . . . Using the golden scrubbing brush, I cleanse my heart. As I scrub the inside of my heart, I tell myself, I am washing away the fear, anger, procrastination, my rebellious nature, and whatever else comes to mind. I wash the inside and the outside of my heart, then rinse it under an opalescent colored water. . . . At first the water is dark, with thick sediment running from my heart. . . . I continue to rinse my heart until the water runs clear. As my heart is being rinsed, not only are the debris and soap rinsed away, but my heart is healed at the same time. My heart is still wet with the healing water as I zip it up and place it in my chest . . . then I zip up my chest . . . the zippers disappear, and my body feels lighter, brighter, and cleaner. I count to five to end the visualization and open my eyes. I repeated this visualization daily, three times a day for awhile.

Another visualization I used to rid myself of anger and rage takes place in cartoonland. I like to use cartoonland because difficult events and happenings in cartoons aren't real; they are imaginary. Villains are killed, bombed, smashed, and annihilated in many different ways. They always come back to life as if nothing happened to them. It's a fun way to rid yourself of anger, and it works!

Begin each visualization with your intention, or the reason why you are doing the exercise. The intention of my previous visualization was to rid my heart of all lingering anger and depleting emotions. I was not wishing or wanting to harm anyone. This is a very important step in visualizing. It tells your whole being what your purpose is and what you expect to accomplish.

To start a visualization, state your intention . . . to release your anger. Then take three out-breaths (count only the exhalations). You are now in the correct mind-set. In your mind's eye, step into cartoonland and find yourself on a desert road as the road runner. The wily coyote or coyotes wear the faces of the people you're angry with. Lead your coyote to the edge of a cliff, and jump off the cliff. Magically, you land on a ledge just below the surface. The coyote runs off the cliff and drops into a deep canyon. Jump from the ledge back up to the top of the canyon, look down, and see the outline of the coyote on the floor of the canyon. You, the road runner, run down the road and find that the coyote has magically returned. He's coming after you again. You run into the desert, find the nearest railroad track, and run down the track with your coyote—or person you're angry with—chasing after you. A train comes barreling down the track. Jump out of the way at the last possible minute, while the train runs over your coyote. Turn and look at your coyote lying all smashed on the track. End your visualization with a count of five and open your eyes.

You can run your coyotes into brick walls, run them over with a steam roller, blast them high into the sky with a bomb, or whatever other scene comes to mind. Nothing in cartoon-land is real, except the emotion that you release. Use your favorite cartoon characters; it will be more personal if you do. The more personal, the more the visualization touches your inner self.

This visualization really helped me get the anger outside of myself. After I've done this visualization in a workshop, I'm often asked what this does to our consciousness, or if this is negative. I think of it as an exercise to rid myself of anger. To begin each visualization, you are required to state your intention to receive maximum benefit. It's the stated intention that sets the outcome of each visualization. I'm not wishing or praying for these things to happen to the people I'm angry with. I'm simply putting the anger that is in my heart outside of me. My consciousness isn't left with the anger, but with relief as I release the anger. Remember, **your stated intention is what really takes place during an exercise like this,** not the scenes in the visualization. For me the first and most important step to forgiving is to get rid of the anger. The ability to release the anger helps me to release this depleting emotion from my heart. When we carry a depleting emotion like anger for a long period of time, it festers like a boil.

The cartoonland visualizations have been fun exercises to do in workshops—people seem to enjoy them. Many say it was surprising how much relief they felt. In doing this type of exercise we get in touch with one of the joys of childhood, our imagination. Childhood was a time when we used our imagination actively. Could this be a part of being like a little child in order to enter the kingdom of heaven? I don't think we can enter the kingdom of heaven with an overload of anger and long-held fears, do you?

Another visualization that I've used to rid myself of erroneous beliefs, and which I've used in workshops, is called "Clearing Away Old Myths." I see myself entering my local library. I look for the sign that reads, MYTH and LEGEND. In this section of the library I search the bookshelves looking for a book with the title, *My Personal, Cultural, and Historical Myths* by Annie Kirkwood. When using this visualization, you will insert your name as the author. As I hold the book in my hands I notice it is old . . . very, very old; its pages are yellowed and crumbly. I've held these myths over many lifetimes, and they cover more than I care to know. As I look at the table of contents, I find my myths on love, spirituality, career, family, gender, sexuality, recreation, money, and every area of my life. I carry the book through the library looking for a sign that reads, "Old, Obsolete Books." I place my book of myths on the shelf under the sign that reads, "TO BE DESTROYED TODAY." Then I walk out of the library feeling uplifted, unbound, and totally free! This has been a very good visualization for me to use to begin to change my beliefs.

You can use your visualizations to rid your heart of lingering anger and long-held fears, reconcile with family and/or friends, heal physical ailments, bring harmony to your soul, love and forgive people, and to relieve pain. Doing a visualization takes only a few minutes and can be done almost anywhere. I've been able to visualize in busy airports, while riding in a car, as well as at home. I do not suggest you visualize while operating machinery; it could be dangerous to you and others. When I'm in a busy and crowded place and find myself reacting in anger, I use a visualization of putting out a fire (anger), and this quickly brings calmness to my heart.

Today I use visualizations to help me have confidence and to stop feeling anxious about a situation. I get uptight when I get around certain family members. Before I see them, I visualize us meeting with lots of smiles and feeling lots of love. In other words, I see us together as I would like for us to be. Most often, our time together has been just as wonderful as I visualized it. I also use visualizations before I travel and for any situation in which I need a little more confidence, a little more calmness, or a little more motivation.

The use of meditation is another very good way to help you rid yourself of any anger, fear, or other depleting emotion. Mother Mary calls them depleting emotions and She is right. Think about the last time you were in a snit. After it was over, didn't you feel drained of energy? There are many depleting emotions besides anger and fear. There is envy, jealousy, resentment, criticism, shame, guilt, greed, cruelty, violence, addictions, and intolerance. These kinds of emotions zap our strength, energy, and attention. They take up our time, attention, and pull our awareness away from love and forgiveness.

You may need help when you begin to meditate. Try different things to help you: use commercially taped guided meditations, the repetition of a sound or word, sitting in silence, or you can create your own guided meditation tapes. I've found that my own guided meditation helps me the most. One of my favorite self-guided meditations is to visit the Temple of Love in my mind. I guide myself to the Temple of Love where I'm able to lay on the altar all my lingering fears and unresolved angers, and relieve myself of inner turmoil. My Temple of Love has a huge trash can on the outer porch where I place the garbage of fear, anger, and all the other bad feelings I can think of . . . what's left is placed on the altar. A funny thing—not the ha-ha kind of funny but the ironic type—is that no matter how much garbage I place in the trash can, as I approach the altar, more comes to mind—other incidents, other people, and other times I had let myself down, someone who hurt me, or someone I've hurt.

You can learn to guide yourself in your own meditation. I talk myself through the meditation as if I were guiding a group and say the words in my mind. First, I talk myself into a state of relaxation by seeing myself take "breaths of light." As the breath is inhaled, I send it to my feet and let the light explode into tiny little lights that illumine every cell, turning all darkness to light, and sending all stress and tension fleeing. I allow the light to spread throughout my body and, as it does, my body becomes very, very relaxed. Then I see an opening and follow that opening to my temple, or whatever other scene I need for my meditation. I always allow time in meditation for total silence.

I've used all kinds of methods to learn to love myself. It took time, prayer, effort, and commitment. I followed my inner guidance when I was confused about a method. It takes more than reading about it; it takes action. I often tell people,

"Do what you can, even if it's wrong. God sees your effort and leads you to the people, books, seminars, or groups that will help you the most. But if you do nothing, there is nothing for God to work with." Over and over I am told that **God only works through us . . . not for us.**

As an example, when I first began the process of learning to love myself, I couldn't find a way to do it. What I could clearly see was my son, who was an active alcoholic at the time. One day I called Alcoholics Anonymous and said, "I have a son who is an alcoholic and I want to know how to get him to stop drinking." Without missing a beat the man replied, "Attend Al-Anon." He then gave me several locations and meeting times to choose from.

I've related this experience in the book, *Instructions for the Soul* (Kirkwood, 1997), so here I will just lightly touch on it. It was quite a challenge to attend Al-Anon meetings due to my agoraphobia. When I attended, I learned what a raging co-dependent I was and how I hid my true feelings. I learned that the reason I could see what others were doing to harm themselves was because it hurt to look at my own "stuff." I also received many ideas, mottos, and inspirations that helped me in the process of learning to love myself. I believe in the 12-step program's effectiveness and recommend it. Yet in my experience, there came a time to put my issues to rest and be done with it. Whenever I have a need, and I "know" deep within when the need is there, I return to either Al-Anon or Incest Anonymous.

I think our American culture is "co-dependent." It seems to me that America runs around the world, telling other nations how they should act, what they should do, and how they should do it. We define "good and proper" according to our standards and often think of people in other cultures as backward and needy. We think America has all the answers. Yet we have so many problems we can't seem to do anything about. Because of this I encourage people, who are so busy doing for others that they have lost sight of their own life, to go to Co-Dependents Anonymous.*

In the meantime . . . after years of prayer and one year of his own daily prayer for courage, my son entered a rehab hospital and began his own healing program. During his month in the hospital, a "family week" was held, and we were encouraged to attend. It was a week where several families of people in the rehab program stayed in the hospital and were given five days of intensive counseling. It was during this week that I came face-to-face with my core issue. This core issue had formed the background for my beliefs and myths. My history of childhood sexual abuse was the main reason I had a difficult time loving myself. After that week, I went back into therapy with the added commitment to do everything I needed to heal the pain and learn new behaviors. Learning to love myself was one of the new behaviors I learned.

Love As an Energy

As mentioned earlier, I had already looked up the definition of love in the dictionary. It just felt right to find all the definitions of energy. I knew what it was, but could not recall all that energy is, so I searched the dictionary for definitions.

---

*Look in the Yellow Pages of the Telephone Directory for a way to contact your local 12-step support group. If you cannot find CO-DA listed, call an AA chapter.

The definition of "energy" in *The American College Dictionary* is "capacity or habit of vigorous activity, the actual exertion of power, activity or force." This caused me to think of activities that would best represent love as an energy: a mother's efforts in caring for her family . . . a father working overtime, or working two jobs to provide for his family . . . the effort of a dedicated teacher . . . a minister as he comforts a family in times of sadness . . . the efforts of volunteers, like the Foster Grandmothers, or volunteer firefighters . . . a friend who is there to hold a hand, wipe a tear, or share a joyful experience . . . a stranger who stops to help at the site of an accident . . . the person who helps a lost child find his/her parents. These are activities in which energy is used in love, for love, and with love.

Mother Mary says love is an energy like light (Kirkwood, 1994, p. 105). This means that love can be harnessed, and sometime in the future we will be able to use it as we do light. In *Mary's Message to the World,* She says we will be able to warm our homes, light our cities, and use it to heal our bodies. I can attest to love's ability to heal your heart. Because I learned to accept God's love and found an inner love for my life, I can say that my heart has been healed. My marriage has been enhanced, and my relationship with my children is so much more open and loving. Love's energy can be felt, like a warm glow on your skin.

In my workshops, and at times when I am speaking to a group, I use an exercise to allow people to *feel the energy of love.* In small groups we stand and hold hands forming a circle. Then one or two people at a time take turns standing in the center of the circle. Those of us forming the circle think the thought "unconditional love, unconditional love . . . unconditional love," over and over in our mind. We try to feel as loving as we can. Then we project the thought, "unconditional love," to the people who are in the circle. When I am directing a larger audience, I first ask them to think of the person or people they love most in their life. It could also be that some people love their pets more than people, and this is what brings up a feeling of love easily. If you do this at home, concentrate on the feeling of love that fills you when you are with the person you love most, and then concentrate on your heart area as it feels the emotion. Now begin to think the words, "unconditional love," repeating it over and over, until you are infused with a feeling of total love and peace. In a large audience I ask a quarter of the group to stand and ask the rest of the group to project the thought and feeling of unconditional love towards them. Do this at home with at least one other person so that you can experience the encompassing feeling of love. No matter how large the audience, when I use this exercise, most of the people will experience the energy of love.

This energy can be projected to family members, loved ones, enemies and foes, co-workers and neighbors. You can project love to war-torn areas of the world and into projects you are working on. During the Persian Gulf War, I projected unconditional love towards Saddam Hussein. My reasoning was, if love and peace are the opposites of war and violence, then this is the antidote to war.

God's Love Is Unconditional

When I first learned that God loves us unconditionally, it really floored me. I had been taught to think of God's love as conditional, and God as a very judging Deity who loved to zap people with bad things. From my earliest memories I can remember the words, "Don't do that. God will get mad and cause something bad to happen to you." Or when something bad happened, like a fall or scraped knee, I remember hearing, "See, you must have been a bad little girl, or God wouldn't have done that to you." Exactly who said these things, I don't remember, but the words stuck in my mind. The first time I negated this idea stands out clearly in my mind. It was when I had my first child. As mentioned earlier, Mark was born with Down's Syndrome, and someone told me it must be a punishment from God. My first reaction was, "No!" I couldn't believe that God would punish me by harming an innocent babe. It just didn't make sense that God would hurt someone else to get back at me.

We have many misconceptions about unconditional love. It isn't a wimpy kind of love. I call it tough love. When you learn to love yourself unconditionally, and learn to care for yourself and set boundaries, often your loved ones will say, "What's happened to you? I thought you loved me"— that is, if you have a dysfunctional relationship. But what they are really finding is that I can't be manipulated or maneuvered to do what they want. When you must act a certain way in order for your loved ones to feel loved, you "know" this love is conditional. To me, unconditional love makes me responsible for myself, but it also frees me from taking on someone else's responsibilities. I can see that God loves them and created in them all they need in order to live their lives free of my interference.

Unconditional love means that no matter what we do, or don't do . . . no matter who we are . . . no matter what condition we find ourselves in . . . no matter how we think or don't think . . . no matter if we are rich or poor, educated or not, sweet-tempered or mean-spirited, polite or rude, clean or dirty . . . God loves us, and this is how we are to love ourselves, if we want to heal. God will not turn away from us. Many times, when I was learning this lesson and thought I was such a bad person, Jesus would say to me through my mind, "Remember the prodigal son. His father kept on loving him and welcomed him home with a feast. This is you!"

There are many misconceptions about unconditional love. In talking to people across the country, it seems that many of us hold the same misconceptions. One is that loving unconditionally allows people to do anything they want to us, and we take it. In some of my talks on love, I say, to love your family and/or friends unconditionally means you reserve all judgment, but you love yourself unconditionally first and take care of yourself first. For instance, if your loved one is angry and acting out his anger by shouting or throwing things at you, unconditional love says, you love yourself and take care of you first.

There are many reasons and benefits to loving ourselves. As I was learning to love myself unconditionally, the realization came that I was practicing on me. One reason to learn to love yourself is so that later you'll know how to love others unconditionally. Another benefit is that it gives us the ability to recognize unconditional love. Due to my history of childhood sexual abuse and other early situations, I didn't know what love was or how to give it. Then the myths I'd built up in my mind further added to my inability to recognize love. I thought I was loving, when in reality I was meddling and obsessing.

When I love myself unconditionally, I'm acknowledging God's love and showing him how much I appreciate His love. One train of thought that kept recurring, "**If God loves unconditionally, who am I to do otherwise?** Do I think I'm better than God? NO! So why don't I follow Him in spirit and in truth, and learn to love myself, my family, and everyone unconditionally, as He does." I remembered a Bible verse that says, "You have heard that it was said, 'Love your neighbor and hate your enemy.' But I tell you: Love your enemies and pray for those who persecute you, that you may be sons of your Father in Heaven. He causes his sun to rise on the evil and the good, and sends rain on the righteous and the unrighteous." (Matthew 5:43-45) I decided that I couldn't do anything else, except learn to love unconditionally.

If you feel you would like to learn to love unconditionally, make a commitment today, and begin with yourself. Why learn to love yourself first? Because it will give you the ability to recognize unconditional love and to experience it for yourself. Then you know the difference between conditional, manipulative love, and unconditional love. It feels so good, you will want everyone to feel this way.

Many of us were raised in environments that taught us to love conditionally. Sometimes parents use conditional, or manipulative love, without realizing it, thinking only they want us to do better than they did. For example, my mother continuously pointed out the mistakes we made as children. Even when we did something good, she never gave praise without letting us know how we could have done better. She thought she was being helpful. When we did something very well, won a prize, or performed well on a recital, she would say, "That was good . . . but, you could have done better, or this little detail was off, or I heard you hit a wrong note." She didn't want us to get the "big head" (her words), so she searched until she found something that could have been better. She shared her motivation with me only as an adult. I can tell you, however, that what happened to me as a child erased the good feeling of winning and performing well and made me feel that, no matter how hard I tried, it was never good enough. As an adult I've had a difficult time feeling I was good enough, or that what I did, created, or made was acceptable, even when it was. As a child, if I brought home a report card with more Bs than As, I was told I could do better next time and bring home more As. There was no praise for the As I got or the effort I had made. Now I know that my mother thought only to help me. But it didn't have that affect on me.

Another benefit to loving yourself unconditionally is that you stop berating and beating up on yourself. I was the world's worst, or best, at self-incrimination. Whenever I made a mistake, I instantly sounded like Cinderella's stepmother. I chastised and scolded myself, told myself what a dummy or half-wit I had been, or would call myself names that were derogatory. There was almost a constant on-going dialogue that would browbeat even the strongest and bravest person.

During workshops, many people say they share this trait. They say, "I do that." Today I seldom berate or chastise myself. When I do, the thought comes, "Stop—you love yourself unconditionally now, as God loves you. You made a mistake, get over it, do what you can to correct it, and let it go." The last part I repeat over and over, until I can let it go. At times this process takes a while. If I find that I can't let it go, then I do other exercises that help. I write about the experience, what is commonly called "journaling." If I feel that I hurt someone, I will write to them, asking for forgiveness; sometimes I mail it and sometimes I don't. It depends on the situation, or person, and if my guidance leads me to believe it will help or hinder the situation. I sometimes talk to a trusted friend, who helps me see the truth in the situation. I look for a friend who isn't afraid or shy about telling me when I'm wrong, misguided, or misunderstanding.

But usually if I feel hurt, there is pain and anger which must be released. So when there is anger, I write a letter expressing any anger, and then burn it with this prayer: "As the paper and words are turned to smoke and ashes, please, God, turn my pain and anger to love and forgiveness."

When I first began to put Mother Mary's words into effect in my life, I had to fully realize how much God loves and how truly unconditional His love is. We can say the words, "God loves unconditionally," but until you experiences this, it really is only so many words. In order to have people get a glimpse of His beautiful, fulfilling, unconditional love, I share a poem that came about through my affirmations and the words that were given to me in my mind. This poem was first printed in the book, *Messages to Our Family* (Kirkwood, 1994). It was reprinted in *Instructions for the Soul*. Because it speaks so eloquently of God's love, I can't leave it out of this book about love.

God Loves Me, Just As I Am

As I kneel at the altar in prayer, God loves me.
If I'm sitting in a jail cell, God loves me.
As I'm caring for the sick, God loves me.
If I'm out robbing and stealing, God loves me.
When I'm happy, God loves me.
When I'm sad, God loves me.

When I'm angry and loud, God loves me.
When I'm calm and serene, God loves me.
When I'm abused, God loves me.
As I'm abusive to others, God loves me.
If I'm in bed with a disease, God loves me.
When I'm healthy and fit, God loves me.
If I'm poor, God loves me.
If I'm out of work, God loves me.
When I'm earning large sums of money, God loves
    me.
When I'm winning in life, God loves me.
When I think I'm losing, God loves me.
When I'm frustrated and resentful, God loves me.
As I remain in a state of prayer, God loves me.
When I'm depressed and feeling low, God loves me.
When I'm in a good mood, God loves me.
No matter where I am—or who I am—or how I am—
    or what I am—God loves me with a love that is
    immeasurable and unlimited.
I AM LOVED, JUST AS I AM!

At different times I use these different thoughts as
affirmations, as a reminder that God loves me, especially
when I am angry, depressed, or ill. It's a good way for me to
keep my mind on God's unconditional love, instead of the
depleting emotion that overwhelms me.

The following is an exercise I use in workshops, that uses
the main phrase of this poem. Do this exercise with another
person to get the full benefit of hearing the words spoken by
another voice. Or, if you are doing this at home, use a mirror
and look into your eyes as you speak.

Take a sheet of paper and draw a line vertically down the middle of the page. On one side, list the things you like about yourself, and on the opposite side, list the things you don't like. Many people can fill the "don't like" side with ease and work hard to find four or five things they do like. Think of the things you have received compliments on . . . like your cooking, gardening, fishing, or how well you drive a car. Anything you do well can be what you like about yourself. Of course, both you and your partner will have made your own list. Now looking into each other's eyes, one person reads three things from their list, one at a time. Each time a "like" is read, the partner responds with "God loves you just as you are." Then read your "don't like" list, and the partner responds with "God loves you just as you are." Read and respond to three things you like and three things you don't like. Then do the exercise for your partner. But remember to look into each other's eyes as you say, "God loves you just as you are."

After doing this exercise, people often comment that they felt something deep within them. I had a person in a workshop one day who was skeptical, resistant, and thought he had already learned this and didn't need to do it. But after the exercise, he was pleasantly surprised that he felt something shift inside him. There was that "uh-huh!" that comes with added awareness. A couple of ladies said they couldn't think of anything that they disliked about themselves and thought this was an exercise for beginners, since they already loved themselves. They too were quite surprised and elated when they had a special feeling or awareness. It was one of those elusive things that can happen when spirit comes into your heart with a gift of recognition. I'm encouraging you to do this exercise; if need be, do it repeatedly, until you can truly realize that God loves all of us without limit or condition.

On another sheet of paper, use the virtues and failings that you just listed as the things you like and dislike about yourself, and create an affirmation ending with "God loves me." As an example, if you had listed on the "Don't like" side, "grumpy," write out your affirmation like this. "When I'm grumpy and out of sorts, God loves me." If you had listed your "Like" that you are a good cook, say, "As I'm cooking tasty meals, God loves me." Do this with everything listed on your paper, both the "Don't like" and the "Like" sides. Then read them over and over. Use these thoughts as affirmations until you can fully comprehend that, no matter what you think of yourself, or feel, at any given moment in time, God loves you unconditionally.

2

Forgiveness

ORGIVENESS IS AN EXPRESSION OF LOVE. As humans we have many misconceptions concerning forgiveness. This is one area that I'm continually working on. It seems there is something to forgive daily. Before I go to sleep, I try to remember to forgive myself for those pesky little things that happened during the day, that if left unresolved can later add up to bigger things. What I've found out about forgiving is that it isn't something I do once and it's over. It's a conscious action I take over and over. I now call it a process. It takes repeatedly stating the words, thinking about the situation, and making a conscious choice to forgive.

It takes work, effort, and the firm decision to be forgiving. When I first decided to live in an attitude of ready forgiveness, things inside of me began to change. The attitude of being ready to forgive saves one from much grief. Now that I've made the conscious choice to be ready to forgive, I don't linger in anger as long. In fact, before I know it, I'm over the anger, which is really unusual for me, because in the past I could hold on to an anger for years. Sometimes it's difficult to let go of anger because it hooks onto some old hidden, lingering anger. If anger flares up like a flash in the pan, knowing that the choice to forgive has already been made, makes a noticeable difference. This doesn't mean that the anger is always gone instantly, but I begin to calm down once I remember that the choice has been made, and all I need to do now is begin the process of forgiving again.

Not too many years ago, I would harbor my anger and keep it alive by allowing it to breed inside of me with vigor. When someone slighted or hurt me, I would become enraged, many times holding on to it through resentments. I would berate myself and say all kinds of angry, ugly things about me to me, in my mind. As an example, when someone would make me feel vulnerable and unsafe, I would tell myself how foolish and stupid I was for trusting. Then I would recall the times I had trusted and how I was "always" disappointed.

Today I remember that I didn't "always" do anything, and that there were people in my life I could trust. Before my healing had progressed to the point it is today, I lived in a black-and-white world and used absolutes to describe my feelings. What I mean by this is that I thought in terms of right or wrong. Was this action "right" or "wrong"? I also didn't allow for extenuating circumstances. The person I judged, most often, was myself. When I confronted someone, or I described how I felt or acted, I would say, "You/I *always,*" or "You/I *never,*" those types of statements.

Forgiveness not only takes commitment, it is clearly a choice. It is a choice we make every day, each time our feelings are hurt, we are disappointed, or disillusioned. Choosing forgiveness has a multitude of benefits and makes life easier and much more pleasant. Once you've forgiven yourself, it really is so much easier to forgive others. The forgiveness of oneself is an on-going process. It's something I try to remember to do weekly, at the very least, although daily is better.

For many years, before I remembered why, I hated a close family member. In a part of my dim memory, I knew he was one of my abusers, but still the hatred I felt didn't seem to fit the memory or be justified. At the same time . . . I had, and didn't have, clear memory of the abuse. I grew up feeling an intense, unexplainable hatred for this person. Because I felt such an intense hatred, it furthered the idea in my mind of how "bad" I was. It was a complete mystery to me why I felt so much hatred toward him. I was taught, and believed, that I was supposed to love my family members. He was the person who I had the most difficulty forgiving, because I couldn't even like him, or anything about him. It took a tremendous amount of work and prayer to be able to forgive this particular family member.

Today he is forgiven . . . without any reservation. The day I could say, "I love you," and not feel reluctant or queasy, then I knew I meant it and that without a doubt all the forgiveness was complete, done, finished. I now look into his eyes and no longer remember any of the abuse, or feel any bad feelings that previously sprang up within me. Each person and each time I've had to forgive makes me aware that this is truly a process; it takes repeated, intense work to achieve. In order for me to forgive this family member, it took several years of therapy, a huge amount of prayer, an ocean of tears, and lots of effort on my part to finally forgive. As far as forgiveness is concerned, I facetiously say I've had plenty of experience and consider myself an expert. In reality no one is an expert, because each time it's different . . . and each person is a new experience, unlike any other in what it takes to achieve total forgiveness.

As I've related this experience in workshops and lectures, I've been asked, "Just exactly how did you forgive?" First and foremost it took releasing the anger and rage I held towards this family member and towards myself. I did this in many ways. Through therapy I talked about it and was urged to explore the feelings that hurt. I was fortunate to have participated in a therapeutic program specifically for incest.* They educated me in how this experience was continuing to influence me. I was shown that by holding onto this anger and fear all these years, I'd not allowed myself to develop emotionally. In many ways I was emotionally stuck in the time I had been abused, and in those feelings. I was perceiving and judging men by these experiences, through the perceptions of a young child. He was not the only family member to abuse me sexually, but he was the one to whom I directed the rage. The others I excused for some of the silliest reasons. So I talked and talked about it, and brought the memory up in therapy, allowing myself to feel the pain in that safe environment. I was also able to tell my family of origin about it and end the secret. About that time I made the decision and the commitment to end the pain. I surmised that if it took forgiving him and/or anyone else to end the pain, then I would do it. What I wanted most of all was to stop the pain I was feeling, both emotionally and physically. We carry such a deep-seated pain when we refuse to forgive.

---

*Incest Recovery, a United Way agency in Dallas, Texas.

Again I used visualizations. My favorite exercise was to visualize cleansing my heart of pain. In this visualization, I poured healing oils in and over my heart. My all-time favorite visualization was the use of cartoonland to release anger in a fun way. In meditation I went to spots of beauty and asked angels to help me release the anger. In many of these meditations I saw a thick, ugly-looking, dark green slime leave my heart area, dissipating into thin air.

One of the best ways to release painful thoughts or feelings was writing about my pain in a spiral notebook which I called my "journal." Before I wrote, I stated that my intention was to release the pain, anger, and fear through my writings. Then it seemed that the longer I wrote, the more relief I felt.

I also wrote angry letters to my abusers. **DO NOT UNDER ANY CIRCUMSTANCES MAIL THESE LETTERS.** Your whole reason for writing them is to release the pain, to free yourself from the anger. In the early 1980s I'd heard of this method as it was discussed over a coffee break at work. No one really had all the information, but based on that scanty discussion I wrote an angry letter to my sister and mailed it. It took years to heal the breach in our relationship. So once again, let me stress, **do not mail these letters**; they should be destroyed. I prefer to burn them, and I'll explain later the method I use to do this. Be honest while you write your angry letters; let the emotions guide your words; don't censor the letter, neither before or after it's written. I address my letters to the person I am angry with by name. In these letters I told the abuser why I was so very angry about the pain the abuse had caused me, what their abuse was still doing to me, and what I would like to do to them to atone for their abuse. When I finished writing the angry, hate letters,

I'd take them to the kitchen sink and set them on fire. You could also safely burn your letters in a fireplace or a wood stove. But by all means, be very careful when you burn your letters and have water or a fire extinguisher handy. Even today, as I light the fire, I pray, saying words to this effect, "Please God, change my innermost feelings from anger and hatred to love and forgiveness, just as this paper and ink marks are being converted to smoke and ashes." My friend, Anita Marcos, calls this a bowl burning ceremony. She uses a stainless steel bowl, and that's what gave me the idea. It's amazing the sense of relief that comes when all your "bad feelings" have been written out on paper, and you burn it with a prayer. For me, it was not a one time thing. Because I had nurtured a deep pit of anger over many years, I wrote many angry letters, and not only letters but other forms of release, before the pit diminished in size and intensity.

While I was in the most painful part of this healing, I took a seminar on reducing stress. In this seminar we used badminton rackets to beat mattresses as we screamed, thus releasing our anger. One of my favorite ways of releasing pent-up frustration is to scream my head off in the car as I drive on the freeway. It gives an immediate sense of release, especially if you do this when you are the most angry or frustrated. I used this method when I was living in Dallas, Texas. When I drove on the freeways, I would scream out loud and allow the anger to rise from that deep pit. I spoke words to release what I was feeling and, believe me, there were times the language was very colorful and foul. After I'd screamed my anger away, I'd then listen to soothing music as I made my way home.

During the years I've been releasing anger, **I've used whatever method felt right at the time.** This lets your inner guidance lead you to what is correct for you at that particular moment. Since moving to the country, my therapist taught me to throw eggs at trees. *This may not be something you'd want to do in the city.* Check your local ordinances, because I'm talking about a lot of eggs—10 to 30 dozen. If you know someone who lives in the country, it's a good release for anger. You can label some, or all, of the eggs with names, circumstances, or whatever you are angry with. In the country, wild animals eat the splattered eggs and broken shells. It doesn't hurt the environment, and it's a treat for raccoons, possums, and other critters. Of course, I thanked the tree for allowing me to use it as part of my healing. Whatever method you use to release anger, be sure that each time you begin to release, you end with a statement of forgiveness. It can be as simple as, "I forgive you for hurting me and I forgive myself for holding on to the pain." There are many other ways of releasing anger such as: painting, finger painting, exercise, modern dancing, throwing ice cubes on cement, or water balloons, playing an instrument, especially something like the drums. I've found playing the piano helpful. When I'm angry, I play turbulent classical music. Then I play music that is soothing.

Releasing and ridding yourself of anger is really the first step to forgiveness. Before I released the anger, I was just mouthing the words, "I forgive you." Nothing was happening inside of me to change the way I felt. My Mexican grandmother had an adage to denote how sincere someone was. She would say, "They/he/she is talking from the teeth out," meaning that they were not sincere, but giving lip service to the subject. As I thought about my grandmother's saying, I realized that many times I had been saying the words, "I forgive you" from the teeth out. Then came the realization that sometimes this is as far as we can go with this forgiveness issue. We begin by merely saying the words. Later we say the words, *hoping* that one day it will become a reality.

One morning after meditation I realized that for me forgiveness had certain steps. I needed to begin in earnest to release the anger. At first I was just saying the words. But this is what I consider the first step—releasing anger by saying the words, "I forgive you." The second step is saying the words with hope. I was still releasing anger as hope grew. Although I was hopeful that I would get to a place where forgiving was complete, I still had anger to contend with. In this step I said the words, "I forgive you, or please forgive me," as I continued to work through the anger. Step three is saying the words from my head, or mind. This means that I understand it's a good idea to forgive, and I rationalize all the reasons to forgive. I intellectualize all the benefits of forgiving. At this point, forgiveness comes from my head. What I'm really doing is building a case to convince myself to continue to do the work involved in forgiving. I literally talk myself into forgiving. The next step is when it reaches my heart, and I feel the need to forgive because we have already been forgiven by our loving Creator. It becomes a deep yearning to completely forgive this issue. At this point, I found I was tired of wrestling with forgiving this issue and was ready to have it completed. The last step is when I forgive from my solar plexus, heart, and mind. I call this forgiving from a soul level. In forgiving from a soul level, it is complete, done, over.

Only through forgiveness can any of us begin to live in peace. When you can get to the point that you not only want to forgive, but need to forgive for your own well-being, then you will forgive the issues that have caused you pain in the past. When any of us can forgive without reservation, peace will be active in our lives.

While I was working to forgive the abuses in my life, the following are some misconceptions that Mother Mary helped me clear up. She gave me a list of what forgiveness is and is not. This is what Mother Mary says forgiveness is not:

1. Forgiveness does not condone the action or behavior that caused the pain, anger, or fear.
2. It does not in any way deny the action or behavior took place.
3. It most certainly does not absolve the person who caused the pain from their own fate or karma.
4. It does not mean that the pain was not felt.
5. It does not take anything away from you.
6. It does not mean you lose, and it most certainly does not compromise you in any way.

Because Mother Mary gave me these ideas, I learned that many of the concepts on forgiveness I'd been working with were false. This new information eliminated all the reasons I used to justify not forgiving. I believed that, if I forgave my abuser, it condoned the abuse, and that it took some elusive thing away from me. I also had believed that I was losing something if I forgave my abusers. But the really, real, real truth was that what I had believed to be true was false—completely and totally untrue. I couldn't use these excuses any longer. I had to adjust my beliefs, attitudes, and thoughts to change my inner self to agree with this new information.

As mentioned earlier, I got stuck emotionally at the age when I was abused. This means I'd been emotionally functioning at grade school and pre-school level, even though I was a teenager and later an adult. There were many instances when I could function as a mature adult, but certain situations could trigger a childlike response. If you think about it, it's rather silly to think that something could wipe away an incident as if it had never happened.

For many years I was ambivalent about forgiving. Having attended a Southern Baptist Church for 15 years and raised in the United Methodist Church, I'd listened to many sermons on forgiving, how it was the "Christian" thing to do. I took these sermons and Sunday School lessons to heart, but still, I had difficulty letting myself forgive completely. I had often said, "I may forgive, but I'll never forget." I remember thinking, if I forgive them (my abusers), then that meant it hadn't happened, or that it didn't matter. And the pain, fear, and anger did matter to me; in fact, it mattered very much.

I've often thought about the times I'd hurt other people. I justified them by thinking that the offenses I'd committed seemed small compared to the pain and abuse I'd had in my life because someone couldn't keep their pants zipped up. This was just another way of putting off forgiving and making myself feel good.

About this time in my healing, I had many feelings of shame. In reality at times it is still easy to feel shame. What I learned from the Incest Recovery Group was that often the abused child takes on the shame of the situation along with a great sense of responsibility. It's almost like the child feels that it's their fault they were abused. So shame has been difficult to overcome. Even today I can still fall into the feeling of shame, and it is then that I must return to the point of forgiveness again.

Learning the process of forgiving allows me to be more understanding when I ask someone to forgive me and they cannot, or will not do it. I can empathize with their feelings of hurt and indignation. So at this point, I forgive myself for hurting them. I pray that I can learn to be very aware and cognizant that at times everyone carries their feelings on the surface, and feelings can get bruised. My prayer is to learn to be diplomatic and say things in a way that doesn't cause pain. Being diplomatic is still one of the lessons I'm working on.

One thing confused me. The fact that Mother Mary said it doesn't take anything away from you to forgive . . . seemed to be contradictory. I'd been told over and over that it takes away the pain. So why would I be told it doesn't take anything from me? In the past when I couldn't allow myself to forgive, I thought forgiving would take a piece of me and that I would somehow lose. Today it means that forgiveness takes away the pain, and this allows me to feel more of myself and keeps me totally intact. The real me, the inner me, is released to feel love, contentment, peace, joy, and all the good feelings without any pain. What gave me the most comfort was that it didn't mean that I had lost anything.

Let me remind you that all I have to use are my experiences, and so if it seems like I keep harping on abuse, it's because this has been the cause for most of my pain and the main reason to cleanse my heart. In no way am I saying that only my experiences count. I encourage you to continue to release anger and overcome fear. My whole reason to learn to love myself unconditionally, and others as well, has been to be free of inner turmoil and pain. In order to love unconditionally, you must be able to forgive. You can't love unconditionally without forgiving. Unless forgiveness is learned and used, you are still loving conditionally.

Who needs forgiveness the most? YOU! The benefits of freely forgiving yourself and others are many. You free yourself and others from past mistakes. Who hasn't made a mistake? No one, really, we all make mistakes. Forgiveness frees us from holding on to the past, all the old pain and other bad feelings that lock us into conditional love. It stops our mind from building resentments. It clears our heart of pain. It releases us from bondage, and it gives us the ability to love as God does, unconditionally. I think of forgiving as a way to practice unconditional love most clearly.

In reality forgiveness frees us from many feelings that cause us pain. It has freed me of guilt, hostility, resentments, even shame. Shame has been a "biggy" for me. I didn't like being noticed because of my deep feeling of shame. As a child, I thought of myself as being "bad" without any basis. This isn't unusual in an abusive situation. As I said before, the child takes on the responsibility for the abuser, feeling that it's his/her fault that he/she is being abused. The child feels the shame and remorse which rightfully belongs to the abuser. It becomes second-nature for the child to feel shame. As I've forgiven myself and the people who caused the abuse, I've been able to free myself from much of the inhibiting stress of shame. Who I've forgiven the most is *me*. I was the one in need of forgiveness and the one who benefited the most by my being forgiving.

Often someone will say, "I just can't forgive. The whole situation is just too terrible to allow me to forgive." Forgiveness is a conscious act. It's something we do because we choose to. If you don't want to forgive, no one can make you do it. I firmly believe in that old adage, "You can lead a horse to water, but you can't make him drink." I believe that we can compel, urge, and talk someone into saying the words, "I forgive you," but we cannot get into other people's heart and literally make them forgive. It's all up to you. If you feel that you should forgive, for whatever reason, and cannot let go of the pain to do it, I suggest you pray and ask God to help you forgive.

One of the most important things to remember about
forgiveness is that it's a process. You forgive, and then you
forgive, and then you forgive again. The same pain or frustration can come up again and again. You continue to forgive
again and again. While going through the process of forgiving, I recalled how Jesus said we were to forgive seven times
seventy. My interpretation is that you do it until it's done, if
it takes years, months, or simply days. Do it because you
choose to forgive. During the process of forgiving the people
who abused me, I cried out in despair, "Why do I have to
forgive so many times?" The answer surprised me. The
response I heard in my head was, "You forgive for another
time and another place."

As a result of my work with Mother Mary, I truly believe
in reincarnation.* I believe we have lived many times on
earth. I began to think of my life now as a series of lifetimes
on earth. In the back of my mind I knew we lived a life in
spirit, but I did not identify the part of me which is spirit. I
thought of my spirit life as short intervals of time, which were
lived in different time periods, different cultures, and different bodies.

Today I think of my life as an on-going, neverending
stream of life, which I call my life-stream. My life is a neverending stream of life. I am as alive in spirit as I am on earth.
I continue to live wherever I may be in God's creation.
Perhaps I am 20, or 60 billion years old, or more. Who's
counting anyway? And since it isn't convenient for us to carry
all that memory with us while on earth, the things that were
not forgiven in past life experiences (past lives for some

---

*For a better understanding of reincarnation, I recommend the chapter,
"The Spirit of You," in *Mary's Message to the World* (Kirkwood, 1994).

people), are incorporated into this life. Even today we are healing old relationships, as the relationships of former lives are healed by the work we do today. My sense is that we don't have to remember our former lives and all that transpired, or what was left undone or unforgiven. All the issues which need to be healed are carried over into this life and wrapped into what is happening *now*. Thus, we deal with them through the people that are in our life today.

For instance, if you have mother or father issues, you may feel that you've forgiven mom and/or dad; it feels completed. Yet old hurts resurface; you don't understand why your mind is still holding on to them. It's at this time that I feel we begin to forgive the unremembered and un-rememberable times in our past life experiences. This mother and father who are our parents today are not only our mom and dad now, but represent all the parents we have ever had. So to forgive the mom or dad we know today is also forgiving all the moms and dads we have held resentments towards in the past. We are given a multitude of opportunities to heal our relationships where it matters, in our heart of hearts. I don't believe it's necessary to remember all our moms or dads from the past. I can forgive any and all old wounds from the past as I work on the present.

An insight surfaced during the time I was working with the idea of "forgiving for another time and place." I noticed that when I delayed or ignored settling family of origin issues, the same issue was given to me over and over. God gives us many opportunities to clear out old issues. You will find that you meet the same personality type in the person you can't forgive in your workplace, or in neighbors, friends, acquaintances, and, at times, even in a marriage partner. Often I say, if you don't forgive mom or dad, you could marry them, work for them, find them in whatever group you belong to, and you will most likely meet them in your friends. My friend Anita Marcos often says that we play "mirror, mirror on the wall" with each other. We see in each other, and especially in our family of origin, that which we don't want to see in ourselves. So to get on with the fun part of our life, I feel we must settle family of origin issues first. We will settle these, whether we want to or not. Perhaps that is the reason Jesus said we are to forgive seven times seventy.

Mother Mary not only cleared away the misconceptions I had about forgiveness, She told me what forgiveness does:

1. The ability to recognize that an action or word hurt, or disturbed another person.
2. Caring enough to stay aware, to recognize and acknowledge people's feelings.
3. Allowing yourself to be vulnerable and recognizing the vulnerability of others.
4. Giving yourself permission to take a risk, to let go of something, or to risk the anger of the other person when you seek forgiveness from them.
5. Loving enough to put pride aside and say you are sorry.
6. Erases the pain of mistakes, goofs, and errors in order to rekindle love.
7. Frees you from the pain arising from the situation.

Forgiveness is love in expression. It's the function of forgiving that allows us to erase hurts and pains. Forgiveness also heals resentments, grievances, and all manner of things. When we forgive, we not only express our love, but we strengthen our spirit.

Forgiveness is many things, among them the ability to recognize that an action or word hurt or injured someone. When we are aware of other people's feelings, we show that we care. Several years ago we lived for ten months in another state. While there, we made many observations about the people who lived there. At first we thought, "These are very rude people," because they would suddenly stop and form a circle, taking up most of the walking space in the mall. These would be a group of anywhere from five to ten adults and children of all ages. We found out that often these were families who were talking over their choices and reaching a decision, and that every member of the family participated. It seemed there were some very large families, and the larger the family, the larger the circle. Coming from a Hispanic background where one obeyed one's parents, I thought this was a marvelous idea. I could see the benefits children would have in learning to make choices. Our objection was that they didn't appear to be aware that other people were trying to get around them to continue with their shopping.

Also, to our Texas mentality, it seemed they didn't discipline their children. The little ones ran, screamed, and were a disruptive imposition on the rest of the shoppers (from our point of view). Byron made the comment that they weren't actually rude because they weren't aware of anyone else. He said it takes being aware that other people are affected by our behavior in order for an action to be rude. With this past experience in mind, I could see how awareness of other people's feelings is very important.

Forgiveness is also the ability to be open and vulnerable, to acknowledge our vulnerability and the other person's vulnerability. In asking another to forgive you, you open yourself to the risk of rejection and leave yourself open to a verbal attack if they are still angry. Being able to forgive is being okay with this vulnerability. It means you care enough to say you are sorry, feel bad about the situation, and/or made a mistake. It erases mistakes in order to open a place to rekindle love. It eases not only your pain, but hopefully it eases the other person's pain.

Sometimes people in my workshops don't understand one or more of these points. I've been asked, "Don't we always know that we have hurt the other person?" Well, think back; haven't you found out later, usually from someone else, that you said something that offended a loved one, friend, or acquaintance? I know that I have, but then I don't profess to be the most tactful person on earth. There have been times that a new acquaintance, or someone I've just met, says something they don't consider derogatory about Hispanics or Mexicans in general, and their remarks have offended me. My mother was born in Mexico and my grandmother and relatives spoke Spanish. English is my first language, but surprisingly I could always understand Spanish, I just couldn't always speak it. My Mexican heritage is very important to me, and I'm very proud of it. So to hear a remark putting down someone for their heritage can be quite offensive. Then there have been times that people will say things like, "What's wrong with you, are you retarded?" Having a son who is mentally retarded, these kinds of remarks truly offend. We can say things that are offensive and hurtful to others without being aware of what was said, or how offensive it was.

Most of the important issues in my life have come down to forgiveness. Either it's someone I need to forgive, or someone I need to ask forgiveness from. The faster we forgive, the faster we open to the soothing, beneficial effects of forgiveness to our soul and to the situation. I like to think of forgiveness as a fire extinguisher filled with love instead of water or chemicals. It puts out the fire of anger, hurt feelings, and resentments, and leaves the situation and people filled with the soothing effects of love.

Recently, we were expecting friends to arrive for a visit. Since we live so far out in the country, when we know someone is coming, we keep watch. It was raining, further impeding their ability to find us. The phone rang; they thought they were lost. Since they were using their car phone, there was a lot of static and the connection kept breaking up. On the second or third call, I was frantic that we wouldn't help them. Byron was answering the phone and was trying to hear them, and at the same time I hit the panic button and started yelling instructions to him. He couldn't hear them for my loud mouth. Needless to say, tempers flared. He turned to me and said, "The next time the phone rings, you answer and I'll stand back and criticize." I went into the bedroom and thought about that. My intention wasn't to criticize but to help. I realized that in the best of times, Byron doesn't like me to talk to him while he is on the phone. It's one of his pet peeves. I told him how sorry I was; when that didn't seem to cool things off, I realized that it would take more from me. I then asked for his forgiveness. It took a while, but by the time our friends arrived, we were on the road to good relations. I wasn't angry but felt very ashamed of myself for "losing it," as my children call those times when I panic.

When our friends arrived, we were still stiff and stifled. But by the time we went to bed, we were reaching out to each other. This is one of the benefits of forgiving. It quenches the fire of anger and lets the relationship begin to heal. I noticed that it helped me get over the shame more quickly and get to a place where I was consciously choosing peace. This time, it was peace in our marriage and relationship.

In my workshops we meditate after we've talked about forgiveness. After having talked about forgiveness, it's time to put what we've learned into action, and a meditation is one way to forgive. For one of my meditations, I return to the Temple of Love (Kirkwood, 1994, p. 198) and allow people quiet time for them to begin the process of forgiveness. It doesn't matter whether the people you are intending to forgive are alive on earth or in spirit. We can still forgive. It's my belief that the energy of love takes our act of forgiveness to the person who is involved, wherever they are in God's creation, and lets them know that a forgiveness is taking place which involves them.

In 1989, while at the rehab hospital during family week, during my son David's stay, one of the ladies attending had a lot of anger towards her dead father. The counselors had her bring a picture of him and place it in an empty chair. She sat across from this chair and talked to him about the anger and hurt he had caused in her life. The rest of us in this group sat around her in a circle of support, neither judging her or her words. She was able to release her anger and let many of the tears loose which had been held in abeyance.

This one incident started me thinking about people who had left this earthly existence. It was then I realized that I believe wholeheartedly that life is eternal. Since this is my belief, I surmised that when I forgive anyone who is dead, or ask them to forgive me, it is done. I believe they know it in their heart and soul. My belief is that when I've completed the process of forgiving, the energy of love takes the message of love and total forgiveness to the people who have passed on from their earthly life. I think they know instantly that the link which bound us together in any painful emotions, situation, or experience is now broken. I believe they know instantly that the fight is over, there is peace between us, and all is forgiven.

I encourage you to forgive and to do it until it is done in your heart, mind, and solar plexus. You will know when you reach this soul level . . . you will know it.

Self-talk and Affirmations

Self-talk is that on-going dialogue that occurs within your mind. To many of us who have, or had, low self-esteem, self-talk just happens. My self-talk sounded like the worst monologue by the stepmother in the fairy tale, Cinderella. I sounded just like Cinderella's stepmother when I talked to myself. I berated, brow-beat, and said the worst kinds of things to myself. If there is one thing I learned, it is to take what I have and use it to better myself. So I took my self-talk and turned it around. I talked to myself as if I were my fairy godmother and encouraged myself to stop verbally beating myself and to concentrate on what I did well. I remembered the song popular in "50s" that said, "count your blessings." I began to count my blessings instead of beating up on myself.

Today, whenever I fall back into old behavior patterns, or old self-talk patterns, I tell myself, "STOP!," especially when it's not the kind of self-talk that generates good feelings. I say to myself, "I no longer talk to myself like this, I'm worthy of being treated kindly."

Listen to your own self-talk. Take notice and be aware of the things you say to yourself when you're angry, fearful, or upset. Your self-talk will reveal where your self-esteem is.

Often I used self-talk to terrorize myself. I was my own worst enemy. I could upset and send myself into panic attacks. I started with, "what if . . ." and then paint dire pictures with words. It didn't take me long to realize that this is not the act of a loving person, especially not the act of someone who is learning to love unconditionally. If this is one of your bad habits, then simply use this same habit to talk yourself into being calm, to uplift your self-esteem, and to build a new image of yourself.

One of the best ways to use self-talk is with affirmations. Affirmations are assertions that something is true. So your affirmations must state what is true for you. Be sure your affirmations are stating truthfully what you want or feel. You must be honest with yourself as you use affirmations. There is no magic in affirmations.

When I first heard about affirmations, I was trying to sell Mary Kay cosmetics in the 1960s. I thought if I said the words, this would magically make circumstances take place that would make me a great saleslady. I was given affirmations that worked for my director, and I faithfully said them as many times a day as she recommended. Nothing happened. I didn't become a good saleslady. In fact, I lost my shirt because I gave away my profits in discounts. I sold at cost to family and friends; this doesn't make you a great salesperson, nor does it make you popular to family and friends.

Affirmations must agree with your truth. Your truth is what you believe about yourself and God. Remember, I said that when I began to work on increasing my self-worth, I used affirmations. But these affirmations had to be true of me at that time. Since I couldn't in good conscience say I was worthy, or of value, I affirmed that I was of value to my children, by name. This I believed with all my heart to be true. The best affirmations are the ones you modify, change, or create for yourself. During the time my Mary Kay director was urging me to use affirmations, I remember sitting in her living room, going through books and copying affirmations without reading the books. One of her favorite authors was Catherine Ponder. I copied many affirmations from her books, repeatedly said them with force, thinking this would help my sales. Never once did I consider changing the words to fit my truth.

These affirmations didn't work because they were not true of me at the time. Just saying words will not change you unless the words speak the truth to your inner being. When you are trying to change your belief, attitude, or truth, it requires speaking your own words of truth. So if, or when, you begin to use affirmations and don't understand how to create affirmations, begin with affirmations you find in books. The key is to modify these words to speak what you believe is going on, with, or in, you today. As an example, "I choose to have a forgiving nature," if that is your choice today.

If you are learning to love yourself unconditionally . . . affirm that to be true now . . . today. Repeat to yourself often, "Today I am learning to love myself unconditionally." It's in the *now* that affirmations work. If you make the statement, "In the future I will love myself," whether the future is tomorrow, next month, or next year, it won't work. In the beginning the best affirmations were my negative self-talk. I turned every negative thought into positive self-talk, by saying, "This is what I am learning now." An example is, "I am learning to love myself, now." I could fall into the "what if's" at the drop of a hat, so I used the negative "what if" and turned it into something positive. For instance, when I would think or say, what if something bad happens, I said instead, what if something wonderful happens and all goes well. This idea was given to me by my husband, Byron. He was the first one to say, "Annie, what if everything goes well, then what will you do?" When I thought, my son or husband is late, what if they had car trouble or they are hurt somewhere or in danger. I changed it to, "What if Byron, James, or Brian are late because they are enjoying the ride, or they are having a good time and forgot to check their watch?"

Begin with what you have, then keep on changing the affirmations and self-talk until you truly love yourself without judgment or condition. You can do it. . . . I'm here to tell you it can be done. I'm doing it, and if I can learn to love myself, then anybody can. There is nothing special about me. I haven't been given any special powers, dispensations, or help. I've had to learn to love myself as best as I could. So my suggestion, if you are learning to love yourself, is to remind yourself daily that all that's required is that you do your best. Only you can determine what your best is. If you don't love yourself unconditionally, you are not qualified to judge what your best is at this time. So don't rate, measure, or predetermine what your best is. Just do what is best today. Forget yesterday; it's not a good measure of what is going on in your life today. Remember that tomorrow never comes. When tomorrow gets here, it's always today.

Commitment

I made a commitment to learn to love myself. Thinking about the commitment was what got me through the tough times. It became a vow and a promise to myself. It was very real. My commitment was to do everything I could to learn to love myself and stop the pain. More than anything else, I wanted to stop hurting and I wanted a happy marriage. I have a good marriage or it wouldn't have withstood the process of healing from my history of childhood sexual abuse. It's been a long, hard road to finally get to a place where I love myself . . . and, most of the time, I love myself unconditionally. Yet my commitment is to myself, for my benefit first, and then for my loved ones. I've often said I would do anything for my children, but this time it was for me. First and foremost, it was for Annie. Not only has my immediate family benefited, but so have my family of origin and my friends.

Recently my sister has found love, late in life. She was ostracized by one of her children. She had been feeling the displeasure of some of our family members. Before she married, I called to say I would be visiting her and hoped to meet her new love. There was a period of total silence on the phone. I could sense her reluctance to introduce me to him. Finally I said to her, "I don't care if he comes from Mars and has purple polka-dots, if you're happy, then I'm happy for you." There was a great sigh of relief which was covered with a short laugh. I feel that my unconditional acceptance and non-judgmental love is doing much towards giving her the assurance that I support her choice. Everyone in our family benefits when we learn to love unconditionally.

Commitment is a pledge, it's a vow, and a promise one makes solemnly. Byron and I lived together without the benefit of marriage for four years before we married. I thought I was committed to him and our relationship. I had decided to live as if we were married, and in my way of thinking it was as good as a marriage. But let me tell you it is not. There is a huge difference in a commitment to be together, and a commitment that requires vows said before God and witnesses, until death do you part. Something inside of me shifted. It was a subtle shift that took place, but it was a definite shift, one that gave a finality to the decision. The choice was made, and this choice went beyond decision to a solemn vow. When I made the commitment to heal my heart of all anger and fear from past abusive experiences, it became as solemn as marriage vows. It took on a life and place in my life of its own. It was impossible to think as I did before the commitment. I no longer could hold old attitudes without that little inner voice reminding me of the commitment I'd made to change from a fear-based to a love-based life.

We make all kinds of commitments, some are solemn and others are not. My father believed his word was his commitment. I remember him saying often, "I have to do this . . . I gave my word." His word was a solemn vow and he took it seriously. Think about the commitment you make to a new company when you are hired on to do a job. There are the commitments we make to church, support groups, clubs, and to family when a child is born. We often make commitments, but most times these commitments are to and for others' benefits. Why not make a commitment to yourself that will benefit not only you, but your loved ones and your community.

There are many ways to make a commitment. It can be made anywhere and in any environment. Before you choose the place or the words, make a decision. I believe that a seriously taken commitment is a soul decision. A soul decision is a decision we make with all our heart, and mind, and from the depth of our being. It's the kind of decision that is so gut-wrenching, and which comes from so deep within us that we are overwhelmed with the certainty that is "right." After the decision has been made from this level, then begin to think how you can solemnize this commitment. I urge people to make it special, like a wedding or christening. If you go to a church regularly and need this environment, then go to church. Remember, this is a vow that is made to yourself and is an agreement between you, God, and your whole self. Pray to get in touch with the truth of your being and with God, then vocalize your commitment. Use your own words, write a script if you need to. Or use your own words as they rise from your heart, and vow to learn to love yourself and continue with this process until the day you can truly love yourself unconditionally. Then vow that you will also learn to love others unconditionally, as you learn to love yourself.

So now you are committed to this process of loving unconditionally. Pray daily, inviting God, your angels, and your highest spirit guides to help. One very important point, **keep quiet about this commitment!** It's important that you use all your energy to forgive, love, and become non-judgmental. If you dissipate your energy by talking about how you are going to learn to love yourself, you will be too tired to do it. When you talk about it with friends and acquaintances, they tend to want to support you, but not understand fully. Or they will say things like, "You seem to like yourself all right, I don't see the problem." Now if you are fortunate enough to have friends who have already learned to love themselves, then these will be good support people. In my observation, I found it works best to keep quiet and pray. Many people, and I used to be this type of person, will talk at length about what they are going to do, then never get around to doing it. I call these people, "I'magonnas." They will tell everyone they meet what they are going to do or not going to do. Yet years later, you will probably find them in the same situation. It wasn't until I learned to keep quiet that I was actually able to accomplish my goal of loving. Now what I've found is that loving myself, or not loving myself, is tied into many other issues, like prosperity, relationships, being able to set boundaries, and caring for my physical well-being and emotional needs. As I go along on this journey of loving unconditionally, I will probably continue to find that self-esteem affects every area of my life. So in learning to love unconditionally, I'm changing my belief system.

I often recall that my inner voice says these words, **God cannot work for you, He can only work through you.** So, please remember that it is with your effort that God will work miracles in your life. I urge people who seek a word of encouragement or advice to "Do something." Just start to move, praying that you will be doing what it is you are supposed to do today. God will take what we do, and if we are going in the wrong direction, He will turn us around without our being aware of it. Earlier, I spoke about how God used my son's alcoholism to help me get to Al-Anon, a place where I was urged to concentrate on my inner self. I visited several different Al-Anon groups because they weren't helping me find the way to get David to stop drinking. It took a while for me to "get" that Al-Anon was not about getting your family member to stop drinking, but to help you see your part in the addiction. It upset me that no one was saying anything about family members who drank, used drugs, or had other addictions. They concentrated on the person attending, not their family member. Also, I needed to find that special Al-Anon group in which I felt connected, safe, and accepted.

It was in Al-Anon that I learned the *Prayer of Serenity:*

"God grant me the serenity to accept the things I cannot change, the courage to change the things I can, and the wisdom to know the difference."

Al-Anon taught me to take care of myself and to resolve old issues. I feel that God took my call to Alcoholics Anonymous for my son and used it to direct me to the "right place" for me at the time. It was the "right" place for me, to seek within my heart and mind.

I continuously remember Mother Mary's words about David coming to our family prayer meetings with his beer. She said, **"Let him come anyway he wants; we will take care of the inside and when the inside is right, the outside will take care of itself."** David and I are living proof of this truth.

Sometimes people call us for a word of comfort or to be encouraged. I find their concentration is still on the outside and not on their inner self. I've had people call to ask, "What can I do? . . . my job is going bad, I work for a very unreasonable person, he is not understanding." Or they complain that their spouse or family doesn't understand what they are feeling. When the focus is on the outside, people want some magical word or phrase to make the other person, or people in the situation, change. They don't see how changing their attitude, or giving in a little, will help the situation.

Recently in a meditation group that meets in my home, I received a change to the *Prayer of Serenity*. In my meditation, I heard the words: "God grant me the serenity to accept the things I cannot change, or *control,* the courage to change the things I can, and the wisdom to know the difference."

Sometimes it's what we can't control that causes us problems and makes us feel we don't have any choices. But I keep in mind that if my concentration is on events, people, or anything outside of me, and not focused on my inner self, then I'm looking in the wrong direction. Outside of me is not where I have control or can affect changes.

I honestly believe that when I stopped meddling and taking responsibility for David's drinking, it caused the full weight of responsibility to fall on his shoulders. This was one of the things that helped him come out of denial. It enabled him to see the truth of his being . . . he had an addiction to alcohol and needed help. When we see the truth of what we are doing to ourselves, we see the truth that sets us free.

During this process, be gentle with yourself. Give yourself the same consideration that you give a baby who is learning to walk. Remember what it was like to learn to drive a car? It seemed there were so many things to think about at once. Then, later, many of these things become second nature and you no longer consciously remember to brake at a yellow light, or slow to a stop. After months or years of driving, you no longer have to remember how to back up a car; you just do it without thinking through the process. This is like learning to love unconditionally. In certain situations you find that you are doing it without forethought. It's just something you do.

A motto I learned in Al-Anon is "one day at a time." I used this phrase while I was learning to love myself and learning to love unconditionally. How I loved myself yesterday is over, it's gone—all I have to work with is today. It's today that counts! If you cannot love yourself one whole day, do it one hour at a time, or one minute at a time. Then begin new each minute, hour, or day. You can only do your best and that is all that is required of you—nothing more and nothing less.

How I used the motto "one day at a time" was that at the end of the day, I gave myself praise. After I had forgiven myself for that day, I said, "I did good today in loving myself." Since harsh self-judgment is one of the things I did, I would say, "Perhaps you could have done better, Annie, but you did good, it was okay, it was your best." Finally, after time, I could say, "You did it; you loved yourself most of the day and it feels good!" Be your own best friend, your own supporter and encourager.

One way to start the day off in a positive mode is to begin the day with a smile, an inner smile. I used to literally sit on the side of my bed, before I got up to begin my day, closed my eyes and smiled. Then I directed my smile to my face, holding that thought for a minute, then doing the same with my heart, chest, stomach, back, limbs, and then into my aura. I surrounded myself in a bubble of light, for protection, nurturing, and for direction. I gave myself a pep talk and encouraged myself to withhold judgment of how I was doing until a later date.

I still begin the day with a meditation. Often I use my Al-Anon meditation book, or one specifically written for incest survivors titled, *Surviving With Serenity*. These inspirational writings help me set the tone for the day. Remind yourself that God loves without limits or conditions. Do something nice for yourself. This could be as simple as taking the time for an extra cup of coffee or wearing a ribbon or a flower in your hair, a new tie, or wearing an article of clothing in your favorite color. You could buy yourself a flower or a balloon at the supermarket, a new blouse, or a new tie. Then do one nice thing for a stranger. It could be a smile, or letting a car in line before you. I like to do nice things for people without giving them the time or opportunity to thank me. It feels good to leave another person feeling good. Send cards to shut-ins or housebound people. There are so many ways to be nice; it's incredible to me that I spent so many years not doing it. More often than I want, I let myself get caught up in the daily routine and forget to send out cards to people or make a telephone call. Writing about this is serving to remind me that it doesn't take much to be kind and to express our love—and to do it now.

In my workshops this is the time to bring things to a close. We end with a love circle. If you have friends who will join you in forming a love circle, it's a good way to experience one. You will be surprised how wonderful it feels for everyone. Just a reminder about how to have a love circle, close your eyes and think the words . . . unconditional love, over and over. In the love circles in the workshops, I ask a couple of people to stand in the center of the circle and simply close their eyes and feel. The rest of us in the circle continue to hold the thought of unconditional love and direct the thought to the center of the circle. We do this until everyone has had the opportunity to experience being in the center of the love circle. The feeling of unconditional love generated in these love circles is absolutely miraculous. Love, then, becomes something that is almost tangible. You can feel it, and it feels wonderful. When everyone has been in the love circle, we end with a group hug. This is a very powerful way to end not only workshops, but meditation groups and other types of group meetings.

Some Final Thoughts

- Daily prayer is essential to your well-being. Pray for yourself and your loved ones.

- If you get an inner urge to go to a bookstore, trust yourself to choose the book that you need that day. Have fun with the experience. Treat yourself like a child choosing a toy. Touch the books, pick them up, read the cover and jacket, feel it, let the book choose you.

- We are entering a time of peace; it's up to each of us to become peaceful and loving. This is not only our goal, but our hope.

- As we change, our family changes; they won't be able to do anything else.

- The only real way to take care of others is to take care of yourself first. This keeps you strong enough to be there and care for your loved ones.

- I believe we chose our family of origin, and as we heal, they heal too. I believe we are here to bring forgiveness and love to those who are our parents, brothers, sisters, aunts, uncles, cousins, and grandparents. We are here to love.

In Closing

I send my love and encouragement to you with every word written. Remember that only you can change your beliefs, habits, and behaviors. Only you can make a difference of this magnitude in your life. It is my prayer that these thoughts will help trigger in you the desire to love yourself and others unconditionally. I realize it is a huge task for some people, and for others who have already been loving themselves, it will be very easy. You have my prayers and support.

I send my love without reservation or asking you to acknowledge it in any way. I hope the information and life experiences I've presented and shared will help you learn to live daily in unconditional love. If I can learn to love myself unconditionally, then I know that anyone can.

Annie Kirkwood

Some Books That Helped Me

Many of things I've used were first taught or learned through the reading of many good books, some of which I've listed in the Bibliography at the end of the book. It was in working with ideas that were first presented in these works that I was able to find a way of changing from a person who lived in fear, to one who is striving to live daily in unconditional love and inner peace.

I thank those untold authors and writers of books unremembered . . . for their contribution and help in my healing . . . and what I hope will be your healing as you learn to love yourself.

PART 2

*Mary's Message
of Love*

Mary's Vignettes

It has been a special blessing to have a part in the dissemination of this information. My prayer, as I prepare to receive messages from the Blessed Mother, is that I get myself out of the way, so that I do not interfere with my beliefs, needs, desires, personality and/or with anything else. Since the beginning I've prayed for God's Truth, remembering that it can be different from race consciousness and mankind's truth.

Annie Kirkwood

You Are Loved

My Dear Children, I want each of you to understand Love. I would have you comprehend that no matter what you believe, think, perceive, or understand . . . you are loved. You are loved not only in your goodness, but your wickedness. You need only ask to be made whole, to set into motion the method of your healing. This healing can take place instantaneously, or be drawn out over months, or years. Your desire to be whole is an instant prayer to our Heavenly Father to come into your awareness. But He will await you making the decision to be healed.

See, dear children, God is always with you. You cannot get away from Him. He is the breath you breathe, the electricity that flows through your brain and heart. He is the movement of your physical body, the impulse to think, the surge that gives rise to your emotions. He is your heartbeat, breathing, inner chemical balance, and your equilibrium. God is your instinct, knowingness, intuition, talents, abilities, intelligence, sensitivity, and your very life force. He is all of these things and more.

Where can you be that God is not? Where can you hide
from God? Where do you go to be away from God? How can
you be out of God's realm? There is no place to hide from
God. He literally hears your every thought, every longing,
and every yen. He knows you so well because He alone knows
your motivations, history, desires, impulses, and your very
consciousness and unconsciousness. **God knows you better
than you know yourself. And . . . He loves you.**

In God's Truth there is only love. Humanity has set up
guidelines for behavior. These guidelines are based on your
belief in good and evil. Humanity designated certain behaviors as good and other behaviors as bad. It did this in order
that you could live together in harmony and have a peaceful
coexistence. Mankind retains the memory, keeps an account,
screams and becomes outraged when these guidelines are
ignored or abused, and demands justice. God has three
requirements: you are to recognize Him and His creation,
return His love, and you are not to abuse anything or anyone
at any time for any reason. Humanity needs these guidelines.
Guidelines are good, they give mankind direction. But sadly,
too many use these guidelines as a way to keep others in
control, bondage, and servitude. Some people and leaders say
you will be outside the love of God if you do these things.
The real Truth, God's Truth, is that you cannot be outside
His love or existence. God is everywhere. He is inside each of
us and He is outside of us. He is the Universe, space, matter
and non-matter. There is no place in His Creation that is
vacant of His presence, or Spirit. Also, God lives within you
and within every cell. God lives within every atom of the
Universe.

God does not require that you call Him by a certain
name. Humanity calls Him by many names, and each name

is good as long as it denotes His true Essence, Creativity, Love, Power, and Goodness, and as long as it is spoken in reverence and respect. Do not become deterred by semantics. Look beyond the word or name to see what it signifies. Look beyond your ideas and concepts of God and realize that no one, neither individual person, organization, or institution can fully comprehend, or fathom, God's Greatness and Caring. Seek then to know God within your heart of hearts where your inner self can truly worship Him in truth and in spirit.

Realize that you alone cannot begin to understand the scope, breadth, or majesty of God's love. It is beyond all understanding, beyond all intelligence on earth, and beyond all earthly perceptions. This Great Spirit, which is God, loves without condition, without judgment, and without reservation. God is loving you now, this minute, in this situation, and in these circumstances.

The sphere, range, and orb of Love is unlimited. It is the Power of God's Love which gives life, hope, and true satisfaction to the soul. This is the love that you so desire and seek through many avenues. Sometimes these avenues are detrimental, and at other times they are merely fruitless and a waste of your energy and time. This is the love which heals, transcends, transforms, and gives life and joy. This Love is Pure Energy. It is more powerful and mightier than the atom. God's love is the clay that He used to create you and your world. It is the atmosphere, ecology, laws of nature and laws of physics. I would have you understand how powerful, how great God's love is today.

My prayer is that you fully begin to comprehend how very much you individually are loved, cared for, and respected. Some of God's gifts to humanity are eternal life, freedom of choice in all matters, and His unlimited and unconditional love and understanding. In His Wisdom He set up certain laws which are immutable. They were set up so that God could relate to you individually and to humanity as it grew. God set up many laws besides the laws of nature and physics. He set up the laws of ecology. Today you talk much about the need to recycle. But God is the Great Recycler. Nothing in nature is wasted. Nothing is refuse, nothing is bad, or truly dead. In nature that which dies simply decomposes. It nurtures and nourishes the whole of nature. Do you think for one moment that God sees or loves you less? Do you think he would not give your death meaning?

God created you out of the clay of His Love, in His image and likeness. Today people think that God created the outer physical form in His image. But the real Truth, God's Truth, is that He created your spirit in His image. He created your essence, your beingness, your life-form in His image. He created that part of you that leaves the body at death in His image. It is the inner man and woman that is created in God's image. It is the part of you that is unseen by the physical eye, but is known by its nature. It is the part of you that thinks, feels, discerns, creates, and loves that is created in God's image.

Begin today, my children, to understand the love of God as it pertains to you personally. Let His love help you in all things and in all ways.

Mary, Mother of Jesus

Love Is More Than
an Emotion

M Y DEAR CHILDREN, love is more than an emotion. It is
action taken with care. It is not only the feeling, but
the thought, the deed, the foresight, and the acknowledgment too. When you love, seek not so much to feel the
emotion, which is at times fleeting, but to be aware of the
deep caring that comes with true love. Loving actions are
needed that will spread love throughout mankind; these
actions are small but they mean so much.

First, begin to act lovingly towards yourself. How can
you acknowledge your life and all the circumstances and
situations that make up your life? Seek to be honest with
yourself and to use true honesty. What is meant by true
honesty is that at times people deny the truth of their
situation to keep themselves from facing some painful or
harmful situations. True honesty is loving, for it keeps you
open to the knowledge that you are important and that your
concerns, activities, thoughts, beliefs and whole beingness is

important. When you love yourself, you treat yourself with care and gentleness, and you will nullify any activity that takes you out of love.

Act as if you matter, because you do. You matter to God, to humanity and to your loved ones. You also matter so much more than you know to the whole of God's creation. You are important, but you lose your importance when you live without love in your heart. Do not confuse mushiness with love, nor confuse romance, lust, or dependency with love. True love is freeing, both to you and to the person you love. True love allows you to be free and the people you love the freedom to be themselves without judgment.

Respect yourself, set standards by which to live your life. Let these standards be standards of unconditional love and ways of peace. Through these types of standards you make a difference in the life of mankind. Respect yourself enough to see to your best interest, to put yourself in good, loving situations, and to keep yourself clear of all lingering fear and unresolved anger. Teach yourself to care for yourself at all times. Speak truth with gentleness and love. Yet respect others just as you would yourself. This is why it is important to treat yourself with love, respect, and peace. The way you treat yourself is the standard you use to treat others.

Set these standards, remembering that each person much set their own standards and live by the inner standard of their life. When you love, you do not impose your set of standards on other people. Yet you live by these standards of loving actions so completely that you are truly an example for others to live by.

Above all, let your words, attitudes, and belief be one based on love. When you do this, you are truly loving as the Father in Heaven loves, without judgment, without limits, and without bounds. This, then, is the way to act in love.

Accept yourself just as you are at this moment in time. Acceptance allows you to open your mind to change. You will want to accept the things of yourself that cannot be changed, such as age, heritage, culture, stature, parentage and such. You will also accept that there are many things you may want to change. It would be easier to change these things if you think of them as each bringing gifts of awareness. Then you will seek to find the gift and to accept the gift with love. When you can accept yourself, then accept others just as they are. This does not mean you must allow them to abuse you or use you. It means that you do not try to change them to your inner set of standards. You simply acknowledge they are different, and these differences give your world color, texture, and pleasure.

Appreciate yourself, your abilities, and your talents. Appreciate the things you do; change the activities that no longer bring you to an inner experience of love and peace. Appreciate your world, the animals, the foliage, the landscape, and the seascapes. Appreciate the beauty that is all around you and in you. This brings more love into the world than you know.

Acknowledge yourself for the life you have lived to this date. Perhaps it could have been different, but do not belabor the past. Leave it in its place and take from the past the lessons learned, the gifts to be treasured, and the memories of loving people and loving experiences. When you are going about your daily activities, acknowledge those people who cross your path. Let them know you see them and are aware of their presence with a smile, or a nod of the head, or with a look of approval. In this way you defuse much of the uncaring that abounds in the world. The inertia, the apathy, will be alleviated with a simple acknowledgment of the person. No great thing, just a smile, a nod of the head. Let these things lead to greater acts of love, allowing the other person to go before you when entering a room or building, or lane on the highway, opening a door, remembering to say "thank you" and "please," and so many other common courtesies that say, "I see you as a fellow human being, a person with your own identity and your own personality."

My loved ones, there are so many ways to be loving. The most important way to love is to support. There are a number of ways to support people. The best way is to pray for them, to support them in their prayers. This means you stand by another person without judgment, because they are important. They may be family, friend, or they may be simply a fellow human in this world. When you cannot support with actions, you can always support with prayer. This is the best way to support people.

Take this message and put it into action in your daily life. Reading about love will never be enough. Speaking about love will not bring love into the world. Only through your actions of love, your prayers, your caring, your support, and your acknowledgment will love spread throughout the world. Love those who do not have love in their hearts for themselves. This is a good way to support them. Love the downtrodden, the hopeless and the despairing. Through your loving actions you will change the world into one of peace and a world where true love and caring are rampant. Live your love through loving actions today.

I am loving you as you learn to love as God does. I know you have the abilities and know-how to put these messages about love into effect in your life.

Mary, Mother of Jesus.

Love Is an Energy

MY DEAR CHILDREN, love is an energy; its properties are such that you have only to think of Divine Love, or Unconditional Love, and you can activate it to a small extent. Use this powerful energy to heal your bodies, your relationships, and your minds. Love will bring more than emotion; it will attract into your life, the people, or places, or methods that will help with your healing. Love's energy can be used effectively to heal family wars, too.

So many families are living in war zones. Brother hates brother, sister is angry with sister, mother fights daughter-in-law, until the children learn warring methods of relating to their fellow humans. Allow God's love to enter your heart and in this way begin to change your family through your example. Also change the family by infusing the members with Divine or Unconditional Love, placing the conflicts in a prayer of love.

Many of you pray for God to change the other person's mind and allow them to agree with you when there is a dispute. Let Love's energy come into disputes to bring understanding in all hearts involved in the situation. Simply by concentrating on unconditional love as you bring the dispute and the people involved in it into your prayers, you bring healing.

Allow unconditional love to help you set your judgments aside. In disputes, there are many aspects involved. It is a matter of compromise, of a joining of spirits in order to bring about a unity of compassion and compromise. In family disputes, there are usually hurt feelings. Unconditional love can soothe away the hurt. As you forgive, you allow unconditional love to enter. When there is no judgment, there is no need to forgive. But until you can reach this level of loving, you need to be forgiving.

Unconditional love opens our minds to solutions, opens us up to negotiation, and compromise. When you use non-judgmental love, there is no need for understanding; it is there. You do not need to have God fill your heart with tolerance, for love is forbearing. You will not need God to fill your mind with compassion, because compassion is a part of love. When you can reach out to a person in unconditional love, there is no need for you to say one word. Allow God's Spirit to infuse the dispute, and bring about a settlement of the issue or issues.

My dear children, I request that you learn to love unconditionally today. Begin the process of learning to love yourself unconditionally and others as well. Forgive and forgive and forgive until there is nothing to forgive. This is how to have love in your life.

Mary, Mother of Jesus.

Love Is Compassionate

MY DEAR CHILDREN, love is compassionate. Compassion is the ability to have mercy for your fellow man. When you are compassionate, you are forbearing in your relationships with people. True compassion allows you to see the other person's pain without becoming caught up in the emotion of the situation. It allows you to be kind in your speaking, to be gentle in helping others, and respectful.

Use compassion daily as you go through routine. At work treat your fellow workers with kindness and compassion. Let your words be truthful and kind. Many people are truthful, but are not kind in stating the truth. Truthfulness is not ruthlessness. Use compassion to state the truth. Let your words bring joy and healing to inflamed situations. Let your thoughts and prayers rise in compassion and truth.

Have pity on the less fortunate. Lift them up in prayer. Let your prayers be filled with compassion and let the pity of your compassion seek ways to help your fellow man. My children, let your help be true help and a salve for your ego. Let the help you give people, help them to help themselves. If you treat the less fortunate as wayward children, that is what they become. They will return again and again, like a child for your help. Then what happens is you become oppressed and find fault with them for not taking care of themselves. When you help, let your help be in the form of teaching them to care for themselves.

Everyone has abilities. When you are compassionate, you see their abilities, you see their talents, you are aware of their capabilities. To be truly compassionate, walk first with them, either physically or mentally. Get to know them and their situation. Allow every person to work to the best of their abilities, realizing that every person on earth has their unique talents, abilities, and capabilities. In this way you see every person as teachable. You will see each one as capable and of value.

Let your compassion help you see people as capable, as having God-given talents, God-given abilities, and God-given rights. Through your compassion, you respect their individuality, the uniqueness that makes them who they are. When you see their individuality and uniqueness, you see their connection to God. For it is through each person's uniqueness and individuality that God connects to that person. In this way you honor God, by honoring every person's connection to Him. I encourage you to live today in love, allowing your compassion to fill your day with kindness.

Mary, Mother of Jesus.

Find the Goodness

MY DEAR CHILDREN, I encourage you to seek within your heart of hearts to find the goodness that lies within. You are made in the image of God. God is good. He gives only that which is good. You have the ability to live and give out of the goodness of your heart. You have this ability because you are created in the image and likeness of God. Only God is truly good. Only God gives true good and only God creates out of His goodness.

Out of the goodness of your heart, you create your life. You do this with your attitudes, your mind set, your thoughts, your words, and your actions. You are not at the mercy of others, for no one can control your thoughts, your attitude, or your mind set. You are responsible for your life. It is through your inner thoughts, your inner self, that you create your life. Your decisions, your commitments, your vows, your own thinking is what you use to create your life. This is a blessing, for no one can take from you your ability to create goodness. No one can enter your mind or your heart and control your true nature. Remember always, that as you think, as you decide, as you commit yourself, you are creating your life.

You are connected to all that God is because of the goodness placed within you by our Father Creator. In your goodness you are capable of being reliable and of responding to your fellow man. Because you are connected to God through His goodness and your goodness, you are genuine. No other person can be you. No other person can do the things you do, think the thoughts you think, or react just like you do. In humanity there are many similarities, but no other person is just like you. You are real. You are genuine. You are worthy because you are connected to He who is real, genuine, and worthy of our highest and greatest honor, God, Creator of heaven and earth.

Seek to find the goodness that is within you and then become aware of the goodness that is within every person. When you are with children, find the goodness within them. Teach the little ones that they have goodness within them. It is a matter of seeking it and allowing the goodness that is within to guide, control, and govern their lives. Teach your children to rely on the goodness of their soul. When they can do this, they will become peaceful and loving in their dealings with others.

Be careful, my children, to honor this goodness, to bless it, and to respect the goodness that is within you. This goodness is within your connection to God. You have goodness because you are one with God. Do not become puffed up with your own importance. Never feel or see yourself as better than others. Always remember that no one is perfect on earth because this is not a world of perfection. It is a world of experience.

Mary, Mother of Jesus.

Mary's Call

M Y DEAR CHILDREN, I call each of you to live a life filled and immersed in love. Let love be the basis for all your thoughts, all your longings, and all your deeds. I speak of unconditional love—love which has no limit, no demands placed on it, and no timetable. My children, love as God loves all of His creation, unconditionally and eternally.

I do not ask more than you can give. You are capable of loving unconditionally because you are a product of God's great love. You were created out of His love and joy. You have all you need within you to live a loving life now. Daily, choose to live surrounded and immersed in God's love. You can choose to live with a heart and mind filled not only with love, but with joy and peace.

Be gentle in your daily life, with yourself, your family, and with all who come into your life. Learn to be kind to yourself, to love yourself without conditions. Accept that you are unique and individual because this is how you were created. Accept that your very individuality makes you precious in God's eyes. Take note of your idiosyncracies; be grateful for the differences which make you unique. Bless your life as it is today. If you choose to make changes, then bless the lessons learned until now. Cease to denigrate or belittle the experiences you have lived through. Love all the events and situations in your life. Blessings flow through the most dreadful circumstances. Dire circumstances can be the most beneficial, when you allow God's love to flow through every event, situation, and condition in your life.

Above all else, love God with your whole heart, your whole mind, and your whole being. Love God because He gives you life, energy, health, and blessings. Love God because He first loved you enough to give you a life in which you are allowed the freedom to choose. He has given each of you talents, abilities, and individuality. Love God in your own way. You may choose to love God through gratitude. You may decide to love God through prayer, or by helping others. Let your life be a loving act of gratitude to God for His love.

It is important for you to connect to God through your daily prayers and meditations. Through your prayers, you open your heart to receive all that God is. Your prayers allow God to work through you. Become quiet and listen to God. Remember that God speaks in a silent voice. He will guide you in all things, when you love Him, and seek His help. God is our Creator. He is our life force. He is the reason you live.

Love every area of your life. Love your frailties and your failings. Love your mistakes and your errors. Love your flaws and your iniquitousness. Love yourself when you feel heartless and when you feel angry. Love yourself when you feel shame and when you feel embarrassment. Love yourself when you are filled with joy and when you are content. Love yourself in all emotional states and in all mental states. Then you will be ready to love your loved ones and your fellow humans just as you love yourself.

My children, I ask you to listen with love-filled ears, look through love-filled eyes, then touch other people in goodwill. Leave off self-judgments and the judging of others. You cannot change the past; it is best to release it. When you reflect upon your past life experiences, do it in love. In this way you will know the truth of your experiences. If there are things in the past that are not resolved, resolve them in love, first by forgiving yourself and then by forgiving all parties involved. Clear away all depleting emotions through forgiveness. Forgive all parties involved in every situation. Ask for forgiveness where it is called for. Forgive anyone who has harmed or wronged you in any way. Live in an attitude of loving forgiveness. Be ready to forgive quickly, harboring no ill will within your heart or mind. Bring peace to the situations that caused conflict. Let your whole motivation be to live a loved-filled life in peace. Be at peace with your past. Be at peace with your life as it is today. Be at peace with your future. Remember always that you love, because God loves you.

My children, I call you to be ambassadors of love. Bring sanity into your world through love. Begin your life as an envoy of love by loving yourself, then you will love others as they deserve to be loved . . . unconditionally. An ambassador of love listens with their whole heart and their whole mind. They pay attention to the person who speaks to them. Ambassadors of love see the whole person, not just the person who is reflected in the body. An ambassador of love sees beyond their frailties and their biases. He or she recognizes that they, too, are children of a loving God. An ambassador of love recognizes that other people have freedom of choice and honors their choices even when they don't agree.

Be a true ambassador of love, by living your life in such a way that only God's unconditional love is reflected through you. When you make the decision to heed this call, you will find the help you need to become a true envoy of love. You begin to change from the inside before you change the outer. Changing in any other way will not bring lasting results. Only when a person changes from the inside out will the results be lasting. When you can love yourself unconditionally, you love your life, your family and your world as God does.

Begin today to change from the inside out, pay attention to your thoughts, biases, and your judgments. Pay attention to what is happening in your heart and mind. Don't be so concerned with correcting your outer life. Take care of the inside and the outside will take care of itself. Spend one hour a day in prayer and meditation. Let the changes come through your prayers, and your guidance come through your meditations.

It is imperative that as an envoy of love you erase all lingering fears and clear away any unresolved angers. You cannot love unconditionally if you hold anything against another person. It is impossible to be completely loving when you fear someone or something. These things must be resolved and taken care of in your own way. Each person will have their own way to clear the unresolved angers and the lingering fears from their heart and mind. Do everything you can to eliminate all envies, jealousies, resentments, pettiness, hatred, greediness, and any emotion that takes your peace from within you.

Then you will be able to love unconditionally, without limit and without measure. Then you become a true ambassador of love, fully capable of living your life in such a way that you are an example of compassion, tenderness, and devotion to God. As an ambassador of love you will begin to allow God's love to be experienced in the world. All the love that ever was is now, and always will be. God does not need to send in more love. He needs more people to live their life reflecting His love. He needs you to be examples of what a person can experience when that person lives in unconditional love.

True ambassadors of love have settled all past issues; they have forgiven everyone who has harmed them; they have made restitution, when possible, to the people they have harmed. True ambassadors of love are slow to judge and, when they do judge, they do so only as it affects their life. As an envoy of love, you are kind in your everyday dealings with people. You are happy and cheerful, because you know for a certainty that you are always loved. You are at peace in your mind and in your heart. Your life reflects that peace as you work and as you play. Truth will be your password and understanding your motto.

Be understanding of your fellow man. Let your heart be tender in dealing with people. As an envoy of love, it is up to you to be the first to understand, the first to find a middle ground where there are differences. You are the first to forgive. Speak your words with gentleness and, even in your passions, be kind and quick to listen. You are now commissioned to be tender, kind, empathetic, benevolent, and friendly. It is up to you to open lines of communication where needed. You are now responsible for responding in a tender manner.

There is much for you to learn. While you learn to be
ambassadors of love, be gentle with yourselves. Have courage
in dealing with your inner fears and angers. Let your heart
and mind rest in prayer and meditation. You can do this, my
children. You have all the tools, all the knowledge, and all the
means within you to become ambassadors of love and peace.
I have full confidence in your abilities to live your life in love
and in peace today.

Mary, Mother of Jesus.

Appreciate God's Gifts

M<small>Y</small> D<small>EAR</small> C<small>HILDREN</small>, as you understand how great Love is and how powerful God's devotion is to mankind, you will appreciate the gifts that He bestows on all people, regardless of race, creed, heritage, educational, or religious considerations. All people have eternal life and the freedom to choose in all matters. You may wonder why I say this at this time. It is because the one (Annie) who brings this message has prayed diligently for God's almighty Truth and has asked repeatedly to have His Truth supercede any beliefs which may be held by mankind. This opened the way for a more expanded message to be given; it opened the portal for mankind to receive further insights into Spirit. No one, not this messenger, church leaders, government heads, or scholars can understand the greatness and potency of our Creator, God.

There are some erroneous beliefs about eternal life. Many religions teach that to reach God one must obey certain rules. These rules are good, my children, and in no way am I saying to disregard your religious rules. But I would not have you ignore the fact that God lives within you. Therefore, to think that only through strict obedience to rules are you able to reach Him, is not the complete truth. You don't need to reach God, only to become aware of His tenderness within you. You were created in His image which means that you live as God does. When He created mankind in His image, He imbued man with His life, and you live it as God lives, eternally. This is one of the ways God demonstrates His love and deep devotion to His creation. God also imbued man with the energy of love, the pure energy which is demonstrated in mankind through his heart. Every time you love a person, act from your love, talk about your love, or think about another in love, you are activating the energy of love.

Let me explain the energy of love. Think about light and how it too is an energy. Because the energy of light has been harnessed, you have the ability to light your homes, your cities, and your countryside. You use the energy of light* to communicate over great distances, to warm your homes and larger buildings. You use light to keep records and knowledge, to cut away dead body tissue and to perform other kinds of healing. There are many ways you use light today, and there are many ways that light serves mankind. How wondrous the world is today because of the ability to harness, use, and distribute light. Most of your industry and commerce in the world today is available because of the energy of light. **Love is an energy exactly like light.** It too will one day be harnessed and used to further mankind and the world in many new technologies and industries.

One way to use love today is through your minds and hearts, by loving as God does, without condition, judgment,

---

*Light in the form of electricity, radio waves and other forms in the entire electro-magnetic spectrum.

or reservation. You can use love to enhance your life, relationships, homes, family, and work. It requires that you first love yourself unconditionally, without judgment or reservation. What I mean by these words is that you accept yourself just as you are today. Understand that you are continuously growing, improving, and mastering, or you can choose to regress in a backward spiral and lose the capabilities you have. You either go forward or backward; it is up to you. The best way to go forward is to love God above all else, to do this to the best of your abilities, and to love yourself and your neighbor unconditionally. The way to put this knowledge into action is to begin with yourself. Pray daily that you learn to love yourself. Understand that it is not bad to love yourself. Remember that Jesus said, "Love your neighbor as yourself" (Matt. 22:38). If you do not love yourself, how will you love your neighbor? If you do not respect or honor yourself, how will you respect and honor your neighbor? Begin by accepting that you are God's Divine creation, made in His image. Accept that He is within you in so many ways. All that is needed is for you to ask and He will answer.

Then accept and appreciate yourself, your life, body, family, circumstances, and your challenges. This is your life, accept it, appreciate it, cherish it, nurture it, and enjoy it. If there are things in your life that keep you from loving God, then do all you can to remove them, to overcome them, or to eliminate them if they cannot be changed with equanimity. Never overinflate yourself, or think you are better than others. Have respect for God as you change from a fear-generated person to a love-generated person. Become a person who loves without judgment or reservation. Treat yourself well, so that you can treat others as yourself. It is a fallacy to think that you can treat other people better than you treat yourself. It is like saying I can pay you $100.00 dollars, when in actuality you have only $80.00 or $25.00. You cannot pay what you do not have. In the same manner, you cannot give more love, consideration, respect, or acceptance than you have in your heart.

Once you have learned to love yourself, then it is time to accept your family members, just as they are. Remember that God allows each of them the privilege of choosing for themselves in all matters. Respect their likes, decisions, and choices. Often people have problems with family members because they don't approve or agree with something in that person. Also, feelings get hurt because of careless speech. A person says something that inflames, agitates, or incites, and there is a break in the bond of love. This is why it is important for you to love and care for yourself first. Then you will appreciate how it feels to be treated with tenderness and kindness. Once this is learned, then you will find yourself treating others with special consideration because your very nature becomes goodness.

What a different world this will be when people are accepted without reservation. What a wondrous world this will be when individuals seek to be loving instead of hateful, forgiving instead of holding on to grudges, when every person treats themselves and others with charity and integrity. Love, my children, forgive, and honor yourselves and every person's life, choices, decisions, and nature. When you can look past the outer and see into the heart of the person, you will find many commonalities. People have many of the same concerns, wants, needs, and aspirations. You are not too different from each other. Today some people find it easy to treat others without regard to the sanctity of life, or the spirit of the person, because they do not love themselves or respect their life. You can begin to change the face and nature of mankind, now. You can utilize the energy of love and expand its use in the world. You have the capability to change the world. Do it today, do it for your loved ones, do it for mankind. Love yourself, treat yourself with fondness, respect, and tenderness. Then treat all people the same way, regardless of their station, education, race, heritage, or family. Appreciate the humanness of people. Appreciate the situations and circumstances that people choose to live in. Never judge their spirituality, goodness, decisions, or failures. These things are solely between each individual and God.

Seek to behold people as they are, and not as you think they should be. Appreciate the underlying motivations, and when you understand that sometimes people live with many unresolved angers, fears, shame, remorse, envies, jealously, and resentments, you will be able to respect their situations and choices. It is not too difficult to be kind, to love, to forgive. It may seem that it is difficult in the beginning, but in reality it is much easier to love than to hate, and it is so much more gratifying.

Mary, Mother of Jesus.

Love Is Many Things

M Y DEAR CHILDREN, love is many things. It is kindness, gentleness, respect, honor; it is caring, concern, yearning, and passion. It can also be chaos, turmoil, upheaval. Love can be a wrenching emotion and a blissful feeling. How can this be so? When you are planning a wedding, which is the epitome of a love on earth, is it not at times turmoil and chaotic? Yet it is a loving situation. When there is a child with a problem, can it not be upheaval to correct and discipline the child? Yet without the upheaval, they may not grow to be a mature adult living to their full potential. Without the upheaval of correction and discipline the parent is not being a responsible, loving parent. Underlying all problems there can be love. Many times situations need to deteriorate to such an extent that it lies in shambles before people are willing to forgive, change, and work together. Sometimes it takes a breakdown to find that there is love underlying it all. At times it takes anger to begin to react to a situation and set things straight in love.

When a loved one is ill, or living in the throes of an addiction, is it not a wrenching emotion to watch them suffer? Yet this is love. Love can bring tears, as well as laughter. It can bring anger, as well as joy. Loving can be frustrating, as well as serene. Love is an emotion, an energy, a spirit, and a compelling force. Love is so much more than what you had previously believed, because Love is God, and God is unlimited and greater than anything. Loving people are not always smiling, quiet, serene, and agreeable. Love can also be loud, unrelenting, persistent, exciting, passionate, angry at times, but never angry all the time. Love can be many things. What underlies all these emotions, when there is love, is affection, caring, concern, admiration, and respect. When a person reacts in anger, this emotion springs into the situation because of a great concern, affection, and love. Think how you have reacted in the past when a loved one was lost, or you thought they were lost, or late for an appointment. Did you not feel some anger when they were found well and unperturbed? How does a parent react when a child strays from their side and becomes lost? At times doesn't the parent react in anger after they have ascertained that the child is safe and sound? The parent isn't angry because the child is safe; they are upset because the child was lost and the parent felt helpless and scared for the child's safety. When anger springs forth from love, it is never cruel or vicious.

Love as a force can be described as the love some people have today for the planet, and the suffering of its people and animals. There are groups of people who gather together in their love for the earth, people, and animals. Their love becomes a force which is strong and able to move old ways of thinking. They use their energy, time, and money to care for the planet, animals, and its people. Today individuals are doing many things, from cleaning the debris from roadways and rivers, to urging lawmakers to enact laws that protect natural resources. Many more people are making others aware of the danger of devastating the great forests of the world. Groups of people are spending their time caring for hurt animals, or bringing awareness to the plight of endangered species and plants.

Many more people are caring for the underprivileged, the hungry, homeless, sick, and abandoned. The coming together of their love creates a force. It is an army of individuals who so love the planet, its animals, its people, and resources that they are instigating changes. Individual people can be a force in the lives of their loved ones or in the lives of people who they mentor. Parents are a force in the lives of their children. Teachers can be a force in the lives of their students. Spiritual leaders can be a force in the lives of others. Love as a force brings great changes to individuals, groups of people, and to your world.

You can use love in your home to strengthen family ties, to effect changes in the way you relate to your loved ones, and in how they relate to each other. Love can create an environment that allows people to be honest, caring, forgiving, and invigorating. To use love in this way, you will treat your family as you would like to be treated, being quick to forgive, and quicker still to accept each other's decisions, choices, and feelings. You can meditate daily on love, what you know about love, what The Bible or other Holy Books write about love. Then think of the person or persons that you love the most, create the feeling that you have when you are anticipating their arrival, or when you are with them. Use this feeling as a benchmark; gather this feeling in your heart until you feel that it is overwhelming. Take this feeling into your meditation and with imagery see it gather into an orb, a pulsing, vibrating orb of energy. Then fill your being, home, livelihood, and family with this energy. Simply see, in your mind's eye, this energy explode into streams of pulsing light and color that flows from your heart to the hearts of the people you think of, and into the situations that concern you. Speak words of love at this time. During this meditation tell the ones you are thinking of that you love them, are concerned about their welfare, and that you are grateful to God for them.

You can use this mental, heart-felt exercise to renew strained family ties, to invigorate a marriage, to give hope to anyone who is losing hope, to help people in times of illness. You can send this energy force of love to war-torn areas, places of oppression, drought, flood-ridden areas, and to any place and any situation in the world. It is a good way to pray for the world, by meditating and sending love out to all people.

My children, God's love is absolute, non-judgmental, unconditional, and given without reservation or qualification. He loves without hesitation or delay. This is how I pray, that you love yourself and each other. This is the measure you use to love. How many of you can say you love without judgment, limit, condition, reservation, or delay? How many people today love their race, religion, ethnic group, educational ranking, or their nationality more than they do others? They feel it is the only way to be, to rate, and to live. How many believe God loves only their race, religion, or country best? Begin today to eliminate prejudices, biases, and arrogance from your heart. Do this as best you can. There are many ways to eliminate things from your heart. First, I would have you pray. Pray to be guided to the best method for you to eliminate any unwanted condition, bias, hatred, or envy.

Do you forgive easily? God is always forgiving. He forgives instantly. He allows each person to have the freedom not only to choose love, joy, and peace . . . but to choose fear, hatred, and violence. He allows you to choose to be happy or sad. He allows you to work through your addictions, obsessions, and phobias in your own way. He allows each person on earth the right, respect, and honor of living in any condition, any situation, and in, or under, any limit. Remember, my children, that God is always present, always ready to help when you call out to Him, and always has your best interest at heart. Can you say this is the way you love?

In order for you to be loving . . . be forgiving. Forgiveness is very much misunderstood. Forgiveness releases you from the responsibility, pain, remorse, and shame of depleting situations. It brings order and opens doors to healing. Forgiveness does not take anything from you except that which harms you. Forgiveness does not keep the person you forgive from the need to face themselves in truth. Your forgiveness is important to mankind. Love by forgiving all things. You are fully capable of this.

Mary, Mother of Jesus.

Find Your Connection
to God

MY DEAR CHILDREN, I encourage you to infuse and embalm yourself in truth and love. Go within daily. Go within to the place of love, where you are connected to God. It is the only place to find God. This is where you want to take all your concerns and cares. Place them in the loving essence of God.

Expand your concepts of love; for just as humanity has limited God through their preconceived ideas, limited views, and fears, love too has been limited. Love is more than you can fully understand, just as God is more than anyone on earth can fully understand. Love and God are interchangeable terms. God is love because He is the power behind the energy of love. God is peace because He is the serenity behind the calmness of peace. God is joy because He is the elation behind the upliftment of joy. God is good because He is the pure wholeness of good. God is life because He is the force that animates all life. So do not limit God, our Creator, or any of His attributes. Love is therefore powerful, and when it is used to adore, revere, cherish, and to share, it is the pure power of God at work.

This is how to love. Love by revering, cherishing, and sharing the goodness of unconditional love. Love by accepting, appreciating, supporting. Love by seeing the good in everything. Love by seeing the goodness in every person, even those who are lost in hatred, cruelty, violence, and addictions.

When unconditional love underlies anger, chaos, and fear, it returns these conditions to goodness, quickly. Love is the underlying energy that surrounds this world and the entire universe. It is the cohesiveness that keeps the planets in their orbits, the universe orderly, the solar system synchronized. Love is the natural order of the universe. Humanity works hard to stay in fear, to react to life through its anger and fear. It requires more energy to rage than to forgive. It takes more power to stay in anger and violence than to seek peace and comfort. It is your natural desire to enjoy life and find love.

Look at the people who are working so hard to enjoy life. Many look to their addictions to bring enjoyment, others look to their own egotistical ways to bring peace, seeking to have their will enforced without regard to anyone else. These people soon become ill, look old, and depleted. They are more often unhappy, uncomfortable, and without real inner joy. Peace, joy, and love cannot be purchased, nor can it be manufactured by man. Only God provides you with true love and real peace. Only through God's natural enjoyment of life and His own creativity can you find real joy. Only through God's great love can you realize the love your soul desires.

All of this can be found in one place and one place only
. . . it is within you. My son, Jesus, repeatedly stated that the
kingdom of heaven was within you. He was not referring to
the people of his time only. He was saying to humanity, to all
people in any time period . . . the kingdom of heaven is
within you. So many of you seek to find the good you desire
in outer circumstances. You seek the love which soothes the
soul in other people. Too many of you are praying for a
certain person to enter your life as a love object, thinking this
will gain you the love your soul needs. Too many of you have
been seeking love through careers, family, passions, and
dreams, thinking this is where to find the love that nourishes
the soul. The love you seek is found in your heart of hearts. It
is found deep within your spirit.

There is a place deep within where you each are connected to all that is Good, all that is Loving, and all that is
Powerful. It is in this place that you are connected to all that
is Divine, all that is God. In this connection you are whole,
complete, total, and perfect. Because of this connection you
cannot stay in confusion for you are connected to all Knowledge. Through this whole, complete perfection, you are
loving, peaceful, joyful, wise, powerful, strong, respectful of
everything and everyone. The all that I am speaking of is all
that mankind knows and all that mankind is ignorant of.
Within you, is hope, serenity, and truth.

Seek, my children, to find your connection to the Totality, Allness, and Perfection that is God. Because **when you do
find this connection within the core of your being, you find
the meaning of your life, the answer to your questions, the
reason for being.** You will find the underlying love that
animates life, that allows you to see God's Truth, and gives
you the courage to change lingering fear and unresolved

anger to your full, loving potential. Jesus came to show you what your full potential is. You are fully capable of doing all the things that he did while he was on earth. You will be able to raise the dead, heal the sick, clear away blindness, increase your food supplies, walk on water. You will do these things for yourself first, then for those who are not able to live up to their full potential. But you too will remind people that this is their full potential and that they can do these things easily when they find their inner connection and remove all doubt, and remove all depleting emotions from every area of the being.

In order to live as Jesus did, find your connection to all that God is, open to its fullest, and clear away all blocks. Release all barriers from your mind and heart, in order to keep your connection in good working order. Selfishness, greed, and cruelty are some of the main barriers, blocks, and deterrents to having the whole, pure energy of God flowing through you. All depleting emotions and thought patterns create barriers to the flow of God's pure energy. That is why it is so important to concentrate your energies on the emotions and conditions that uplift and bring peace. Foster love within yourself, for yourself and others. It is very important that you resolve all old angers, forgive every person in your life, that you love yourself first, and then others, without limit or condition.

Do you see, my children, that all people have this connection? It is within each of you. You do not need to seek outside of yourself for your connection to God. You cannot provide anyone else with their connection, as theirs too is within their heart of hearts. As you think of your loved ones, remember that they have a place of wholeness where they are connected to the Totality of God. It is your challenge to remember their connection and their ability to have God's pure energy flowing freely in their lives. Do this especially when they forget, indulge in addictions of any kind, and as they fall into fear and unresolved angers. Your ability to remember their connection to the Divine will enable you to truly be of help as they go through life in their own way, at their own pace, and with their own views. This is the true acceptance that comes as love.

Acceptance is love, the acceptance of your own connection to God that gives you the impetus to free yourself and others from your interference. Acceptance goes a long way towards promoting peace. First and foremost is acceptance of yourself, just as you are at this moment. You must accept yourself, just as you are at any given moment in time. When you can accept yourself, your own idiosyncracies, your own way, and your own innate nature, then it will be easier to accept your loved ones and all people. Begin with yourself. Love yourself. Be your own best support. Remember that as you clear your heart of all lingering fears and all unresolved angers, you are promoting peace on earth. Many times people want to have an impact and an influence on the world. **It is through your inner life that you impact and influence the world.** When you change from a person who harbors fear or anger, to one who is forgiving by nature and loving by instinct, then you are doing more to promote peace on earth than all the peace conferences ever held. When the appropriate number of people have inner peace, then peace will spread throughout the world.

God loves unconditionally and that is how I pray that you will learn to love. Unconditional love is a love that remembers the full connection to God that is within each person. Unconditional love frees, liberates; it does not place markers or tags on God's free flowing energy and power. Unconditional love takes responsibility for itself; it doesn't play games, manipulate, or interfere with another person's life goals. Unconditional love says, "I am whole because I am pure energy, powerful, alive, and unlimited." Unconditional love has no strings to attach; it never inhibits, nor does it entangle, or deplete. Unconditional love allows each person to open to as much as they can withstand. As you know, unconditional love is not just sweetness, it is chaos; it is not just meekness, it is upheaval; it is not just gentleness, it can be anger; it is not just kindness, it can be stern; it is not just mildness, it can be unrelenting. Unconditional love is so much more than you had thought it was. When you can love yourself unconditionally, you will find a new strength in your love. As you learn to love others unconditionally, you will hold them responsible for their own lives, their own decisions, and their own plans.

I am talking about adult-to-adult relationships, not the parent-child relationships. Parents with small children, love them unconditionally so that you can teach them to make good decisions. Then allow your minor children to decide according to their abilities, age, and education. You are the educator, you are the teacher, and you are their mentor. See your parental responsibilities in this light. See how it will benefit your children to be loved by a wise parent who knows how to love unconditionally and is willing to love them that way. Love in this instance is freeing both to the child and the parent.

Mary, Mother of Jesus.

Love Is Active

My Dear Children, love is very important to your well-being. It is important to your physical growth. Without love your spiritual development does not take place. To simply think of love, pontificate on love, or see it as an abstract is not enough. Love is active. Actively use love as you deal with people daily. Actively love your family. Love's activity is kindness, forgiveness, trust, loyalty, steadfastness, and caring. To love is to release, free, support, maintain, respect, and honor people and their conditions. Love means you actively engage in your life daily.

When you arise each morning, bless the day. Bless it and pray, giving thanks for your life and for its activities. For through the activities of your day, you are able to love. Through the activities of your work, you have the opportunity to love. Through the activities of inner life, you have the ability to love. Smile more, be cognizant of people, of your surroundings and of your life.

Often people go through the motions of living, but do not actively engage in the activities of the day. They do as little as they can, participate as little as they can, and ignore or neglect themselves and their family. Do not fall into this habit. It only takes a small effort to become more active in your life. It only takes a few changes to have an in-pouring of love from Spirit that will energize you, your daily activities, and your life.

Becoming cognizant of people doesn't mean you take responsibility for them or their happiness. It means you recognize them as human beings. It means you respect their opinions, decisions, and choices. It means you work to cooperate in your mutual endeavors, whether that endeavor is the crossing of a street or creating a community.

When you are with people, look, think, and treat them with acceptance, appreciation, and awareness. Listen to people who speak to you, listen with your whole mind, heart, and spirit. Hear every word they speak. Pay attention to their words, their meaning, and to their spirit. Look into their beautiful faces, showing them that you care, are interested, and that you hear them with your whole being. These are simple ways to love people. If you have not acted or loved in this way before, it may not seem simple, but with practice and time you will be loving actively with every encounter.

Too many people today are not actively living. They go through the motions: they arise in the morning, go to work, do what is required of them for their job, and interact with people superficially. They live in a half-hearted, bored, weary way. If you arise in the morning, without seeing the beauty of the day or your surroundings, you lack love. If you do not interact with the people in your life with interest and enthusiasm, there is a lack of love. Many children today suffer from a lack of attention, acknowledgment, and caring. Parents are too busy with their own activities. If you listen with half an ear to what your children say, or don't hear at all, you are depriving your child of love. Blessed is the child whose parents truly listen, hear, and give their whole heart, mind, and soul.

People are growing up with a lack of love in the form of attention, respect, acknowledgment for their person, thoughts, feelings, dreams, hopes, and spirit. Too often you are not aware of the beauty and love which is your make-up. You create out of what you are. A child who is given unconditional love, feels worthy and of value, and is taught to appreciate, accept, and respect themselves and others, is truly blessed. He matures into a loving, creative, motivated, gentle, peaceful human—one who is worthy of being called a child of God.

In your daily interactions with your loved ones, give your whole attention. It doesn't take much time—it takes your whole mind, thought, and awareness to give loving attention. To give loving attention means that while you converse with that person, you do not think of other things, nor are you doing something else. It also means you look, listen, hear, and are accepting and aware of the person who is speaking to you.

Now, my children, love as God loves, unconditionally and without reservation or limit.

Mary, Mother of Jesus.

Love Sustains the World

M Y DEAR CHILDREN, it is love which sustains this world. Love is the essence of your being. It is love which you seek, when you seek that elusive, fleeting component that you feel is missing from your life. It is love which makes your life worthwhile. It is love which nourishes and provides comfort in life. You need love in order to live a happy, comfortable, and satisfying life.

Love gives meaning to your life. Love may be the love you have for your children, parents, spouse, or country. It does not matter how that love is focused, it only matters that you have love in your life. You need love, not manipulation, or control, or anything else except love. When you love, you have purpose, you find direction, and you have an inner connection to all that is.

Love God first and foremost. This is the way to have a life that is at once satisfying, worthwhile, and filled with purpose.

When you have love in your heart, you have an inner peace and confidence that is deep-felt. It is the only commandment that Jesus gave to you. He said, "To love God with all your heart, all your mind, and all that you are." God loves each of you in this way, with His Whole Entire Being. He loves without condition, judgment, limit, without measuring, or rating you in any way. God loves us in ways that are not yet revealed. He loves us enough to trust us to realize that we are better because of His love. **God loves each person on earth whether they understand it or not. He loves each person whether they are worthy or not.**

His love is such that He allows you to make mistakes, to turn away from Him if you so choose. He allows people the freedom to choose what and how they will live their life. God glories in your accomplishments. He would prefer you to love, forgive, and live in peace. He delights in your progress as you forgive family, yourself, friends and acquaintances. He basks in the atmosphere of your inner peace. He adores the way you struggle to find your own unique way to Him. He is always ready to assist you, to come to your aid, and to help you be aware of His presence in your life.

When you fully understand the extent of His great love, you will be comforted, sustained, and motivated to live in peace. When you have touched the inner peace that comes from seeking God, you will desire above all else that every person on earth live in the peace that passes understanding. Love fully comprehended is the freedom to be at peace, to be serene, and to be still.

God's love is not like anything on earth. If you think that God loves as people do, you are in error. God loves much more than humankind is capable of. God's love cannot be compared to anything on earth. The closest comparison is the love a parent feels for his or her child, when that parent loves unconditionally. But even then it is a weak reflection of God's love. Even as a good parent wishes and hopes for good to come to their child, so does God want only good to come to you.

In every event or situation of your life, look for His blessing. When it appears that bad things are happening in your life, seek to find the hidden gift, the blessing that is a part of every situation, every event, every circumstance. My little children, there will always be a blessing of equal or greater value. No event in your life is wasted unless you fail to find the blessing.

Remind yourself daily that you are loved, by a Creator that never sleeps, never slumbers, and never tires. He is constantly aware of your every need. He waits for you to call upon Him to help. Remember that God can and does help in a multitude of ways, not always as you designate. His greatest joy is in giving. His greatest pleasure is to be of help to you. His greatest love is His creation, which includes you.

Now my children, rest in His love. Be calm in His assurance of hope. Have confidence in His outcome. God knows what is best for you, what will really be of help, and what you truly need. I am loving you as you come into the realization of His great love.

Mary, Mother of Jesus.

You Are a Miracle

M Y DEAR CHILDREN, I've come to make you aware. You are missing so much! At each place of my apparitions, I ask you to pray, to return to God, and to be at peace. I ask you to love as God loves you. Yet you continue to seek miracles and phenomena. You do not recognize the greatest of His miracles—the miracle that is you.

Today . . . this minute as you read, or learn of this message, I would have you understand that you are a miracle. You are phenomenal. Become aware of the miracle of life. Become aware and be awed by the life force that so lovingly animates you. It's God's life that flows through your body, your heart, and your mind. It is God's thoughts that give you direction. It is God's love that motivates you to do good. It is God's joy that brings you true happiness. It is God's energy that moves you. This is the true miracle. It is the miracle that is you.

When you become truly aware of the miracle of your life, you will appreciate it more. You will value your days and the life which you are living. Too often, you sit and bemoan your life. You complain when life does not comply with your selfishness. You feel unloved . . . when Love is within you.

Open your eyes, my little children. Open your eyes to the gifts of God. Open your eyes to the Truth of His Love. You are each precious to Him. Do not waste your life. Do not devalue your worth or your days. Never let yourself forget that the kingdom of heaven is within you. To seek God anywhere else is futile.

Be glad and rejoice, for the miracles you seek are all around you. Miracles are within, because they are you. Become aware of your life. Awaken and realize the love God has for you. Value your life and live to the Glory of God.

Think well of yourself. Realize there is much good in your life. Concentrate on your goodness . . . live up to it, and you please God. Speak well of yourself, not overinflating your importance, nor condemning your existence. Please God by living as if there is only goodness in the world. Set your sights on the goodness within your loved ones. Recognize that within each person is the goodness of God. When your loved ones disappoint you, search the goodness within them. When you co-workers ignore and manipulate you, seek the goodness within them. When you are battered by the circumstances of your life, seek the good in those very circumstances. You will find more good than you expect.

Each of you has freedom of choice; it is a gift of God. You are free to be, to act, to think, and to live as you desire. You can concentrate on the goodness within yourself and within others, or you can choose to ignore it. You can choose to bring more goodness into the world, or you can become apathetic. You are free to love yourself and your loved ones without strings, or manipulations, or you can be conniving and deceptive. You may choose to bring more love into the world, or add to its chaos.

To live your inner life in peace is to bring peace into your world. To live your life based on unconditional love is to bring more healing into your world. To be more understanding and seek to find ways to compromise is to assist in the real peace movement. To set aside your biases and prejudices is to become more tolerant, and therefore to be more peaceful. Be aware of your potential to assist this world into being the wonderful, peaceful planet it was meant to be.

Correct no one but yourself. Yes, there are many who live in violence, but you do not add peace to the world by judging them, condemning them, or criticizing them. You add peace to the world by living and loving as God does, without judgment and in total unconditional love. I would have you be aware that just as you are a miracle, so is every person on earth—even those who are living and acting from their angers and fears in violence. You help these poor souls through your prayers. You help them by being and living your life as an example. You help your future and the future of your children, and your children's children, by acknowledging the miracle of life.

You are a miracle, you are goodness, you are loved. Of this be assured, for if it were not so, I would have told you.

Mary, Mother of Jesus.

God Is Within

MY DEAR CHILDREN, you are a part of God. As His creation you are infused with His energy. One of the great fallacies of this era is the belief that you are separate and apart from God. You cannot be separated from God, because it is His energy that animates you. It is His impulse that regulates your breathing, heart rate, chemical reactions, and electrical impulses. Nothing happens in your body without the full use of God's Divine energy.

Many people today pray to God as if He were outside of their being. They seek Him through a priest, evangelist, monks, shamans, parents, or other people. My children, if this is the only way you can relate to God, then realize there is a better way. Understand that God is always within you. He is loving you with a love that is unconditional. To look for God outside of yourself is self-defeating and useless. My son, Jesus, told you over 2000 years ago that the kingdom of heaven is within you. He reminded you to seek God in the inner closet of your being. He also said the only commandment was to love God with all your heart, mind, and all that you are.

How can you love God and not His creation? How can you neglect your fellow man in time of anguish? How can you say that you love God, when you are fighting with family members? Loving God is demonstrated through your love for your family, neighbors, and your fellow man. Your family may consist of parents, siblings, grandparents, aunts, uncles, and cousins. It may consist of many more people. So if there is anger or resentments towards any of these people, you cannot say in good conscience that you love God. Loving God requires that you love all the people you are closely related to, and also your neighbors. Your neighbors are not only those people who live in your own neighborhoods, but those people who live in your city, county, province, state, nation and your world. Your neighborhood is global; it includes your whole human family of mankind.

To keep feuds alive with resentments, jealousy, and envies, is to keep your mind and heart closed to God. Only you can separate yourself from God. To remain biased with bigotry and prejudices is to separate yourself from God. To feel that you are better than other people is to separate yourself from God. To believe that your education, financial status, pedigree, or lineage is better than another's is to separate yourself from God. To imagine that you hold more wisdom, knowledge, or intelligence than other people is to separate yourself from God. To believe that your health practices are better than what other people practice is to separate yourself from God. To believe that your prayers, healings, or teachings are better than other people's is to separate yourself from God.

Each person is a unique creation of God. Each culture is imbued with God's wisdom, knowledge, and intelligence. Every race is loved by God. Every talent that people have is a gift from God. Every religion has its truths and is a way to find God in your heart and mind. Seek your similarities and find ways to blend your life with others. Seek the good in others and you find God in them.

My little children, do not think of yourself as anything but a loved creation of a loving and benevolent Creator. You are always in God's presence, surrounded and imbued with His love. You are filled with His energy and maintained in His intelligence. You are to love and forgive as God does . . . unconditionally and joyfully. You can love as God does, you know. You can rid your heart and mind of all that separates you from God. You have all the intelligence, knowledge, and ability to do this. Be loving, my dear ones. Let the goodness that is deep within fill your being with love. Rid your inner self of all unresolved anger, lingering fear, and of the idea that you are separate from God.

Let your inner goodness shine as a beacon of joyful peace. Let your inner self become serene in the awareness that you are a creation of a loving Creator. Allow your inner courage to help you change from a separate, angry, hate-filled person to one who is serene in the knowledge that he or she is loved unconditionally. Allow yourself to love others in this same way. Then you please God. I am loving you with all my heart. I accept you just as you are now. Change the inside, and your outer life will become more loving, peaceful, and joyful.

Mary, Mother of Jesus.

Live in Peace

MY LITTLE CHILDREN, I would not have you be ignorant or misled. I come to you in peace and a heart filled with love. It is my desire that you know the truth, not as mankind knows it, but as God, who created you, me, and all worlds, knows the truth. Where God is, there is only love, peace, joy, knowledge, and an understanding that is beyond anything you know. Nothing that is of God can be anything else. All other attributes associated or designated as being of God are false.

God does not punish, God loves. God does not become angry, you do. God does not impose His will on you; you impose your will on yourself and other fellow men. God does not cause wars, nor does He impress upon people to kill one another. God loves, He is at peace, and wishes you to live in His peace and His joy. God doesn't stir up misunderstandings in order to try you. God understands all of your ways. He knows you better than you know yourself. He sees into your heart of hearts and knows your motivations. God awaits you to seek Him in order to bring into your world His peace, love, and understanding.

God has no reason to cause you evil, or wickedness. These are the workings of mankind. God loves . . . that is all He is and all He does. God lives in you and experiences all that you experience. When you are at war, it is yourself that you fight. When you are in peace, it is in God's peace that you reside. God does not condone the governing of tyrants, not does He desire for His children to live in tyranny. God has given each of you complete freedom over your own life, life-force, and life experiences. It is up to you to bring peace into the world.

You bring peace into the world through becoming peace within yourself. Acknowledge the love that God has for you as you live your life based on love. Forgive as God has already forgiven you. Bring peace into your life, your family, and your area of the world. This is all that is required of you, to love as God loves you, to become peaceful in your own way and to the best of your ability, and to life peaceably every day, not just on holy days or when you are being seen, but to live peaceably within yourself where no one can see.

There are many practical and simple ways to live in peace. First you decide and make the commitment to live in peace—to seek to love where there is no love. Then you find ways to speak in loving and peaceful tones. To let the love and peace which is in your heart shine through your words, and your deeds. If you force yourself to speak in soft, modulated tones, thinking this will bring peace to your heart, you will be dealing falsely with yourself. First you must be at peace in your heart, then your tones and words will reflect the love and peace that is in your heart.

Other practical ways are to find ways to compromise where there seems to be no arena of agreement. Jesus taught you to agree with your adversary quickly while you are still with them. In this way you do not allow anger or hurt feelings to linger and grow. While you are with your adversary, you have the opportunity to dialogue face to face. You have the advantage of using your whole being to listen and to understand.

I urge you, my children, to heed my words, to bring peace and love into your lives in the best way that is available to you. I urge you to fill your prayers with love, to fill your homes with love, and to bring peace into your family. I am praying with you in love and loving you every day of your life.

Mary, Mother of Jesus.

God Lives Within Every Atom

M Y DEAR CHILDREN, God's devotion to mankind is powerful and loving. As you begin to understand this, you will appreciate the gifts He bestows on all people, regardless of race, creed, heritage, educational or religious considerations. All people have eternal life and the freedom to choose in all matters. God is everywhere. He is inside each of us, and He is outside of us. He is the Universe, space, matter and non-matter. There is no place in His Creation that is vacant of His presence, or Spirit. Also, God lives within you and within every cell. God lives within every atom of the Universe and within every atom of your being.

This concept of God living both within every atom of the Universe and living at the same time within every atom of your being is beyond all understanding, beyond all intelligence on earth, and beyond all earthly perceptions. This Great Spirit that loves without condition, judgment, or reservation is loving you this minute, in this situation, and in these circumstances.

God does not require that you call Him by a certain name. Humanity calls Him by many names; each name is good as long as it denotes His true Essence, Creativity, Love, Power, and Goodness, and as long as it is spoken in reverence and respect. Do not become deterred by semantics. Look beyond the word or name to see what it denotes. Look beyond your ideas and concepts of God and realize that no one, neither individual person, organization, or institution can fully comprehend, or fathom God's Greatness and Caring. Seek then to know God within your heart of hearts where your inner self can truly worship Him in truth and in spirit.

Realize that you alone cannot begin to understand the scope, breadth, or majesty of God's love. It is beyond all understanding, beyond all intelligence on earth, and beyond all earthly perceptions. This Great Spirit that loves without condition, without judgment, and without reservation is loving you now, this minute, in this situation, and in these circumstances.

The sphere, range, and orb of Love is unlimited. It is the Power of God's Love which gives life, hope, and true satisfaction to the soul. This is the love that you so desire and seek through many avenues. Sometimes these avenues are detrimental, and at other times they are merely fruitless and a waste of your energy and time. This is the love which heals, transcends, transforms, and gives life and joy. This Love is Pure Energy. It is more powerful and mightier than the atom. God's love is the clay that He used to create you and your world. Love is the atmosphere, ecology, laws of nature and laws of physics. I would have you understand how powerful, how great God's love is today.

God is devoted to you. His devotion is such that He not only allows you to make your choices, but He totally supports your choice. He helps you to make the best of all situations and all choices. God gives freely of Himself that you may have life. You may have this life to live as you so choose. His devotion is that He does not leave you when you turn away from Him. He simply patiently awaits your return to His love. While you turn away from Him, He continues to give you breath to breathe, food to eat, water to quench your thirst, and a world that is beyond beautiful.

My prayer is that you fully begin to comprehend how very much you individually are loved, cared for, and respected. Some of God's gifts to humanity are eternal life, freedom of choice in all matters, and His unlimited and unconditional love and understanding. In His Wisdom He set up certain laws which are immutable. They were set up so that God could relate to you individually and to humanity as it grew. God set up many laws besides the laws of nature and physics. He set up the laws of ecology. Today you talk much about the need to recycle. But God is the Great Recycler. Nothing in nature is wasted. Nothing is refuse, nothing is bad, or truly dead. That which is bad, or dead, simply decomposes. It nurtures and nourishes the whole of nature. Do you think for one moment that God sees or loves you less? Do you think he would not give your death meaning?

Mary, Mother of Jesus.

Love God by
Appreciating Nature

M Y DEAR CHILDREN, you can return God's love in many ways. You can appreciate and care for the forest, the marshlands, the open spaces in nature. You can appreciate and care for His wildlife. In many parts of the world the animals are being thrown out of their natural homes. They are being hunted, not to sustain and nourish man, but to be used as trophies. Mankind is ignoring the animals on earth. The birds are being displaced from their natural homes. You can love God's animals enough to care for them or to help organizations who do care for the animals.

You love God by appreciating nature. You can clean up the waterways and coast lines. You can love the plant life that is within your area. Too many times man appreciates other regions and sees the beauty in other locations. Begin to see the beauty around you. It is through the appreciation of nature that you can love God.

Appreciate your bodies. Too many people today do not appreciate their bodies. They denegrate, neglect and abuse their bodies. Care for your bodies, give them good sustenance and water. Use your body in the way it was created to be used. But also care for your entire being. Take care of your emotions, clear away those emotions that deplete and damage your spirit. Take care of your minds. It is important to learn to think clearly, to use all your intellect and wisdom. You can clear away those thought patterns that damage you and deplete your energy. You can forgive yourself and gain so much energy by releasing any thought or feeling that makes you feel bad. Take care of your spirit. Do not let yourself become dispirited or depressed. Realize that, when you are depressed and feeling low, you are still in God's love.

Appreciate your life. If there are areas that cause you to abuse yourself or anyone else, then do all you can to eliminate those areas, thought patterns, addictions, or whatever it is that keeps you in the abuse. Do all of this to the best of your abilities. Be honest with yourself and stay in the awareness of God's love.

My prayer is that you fully begin to comprehend how very much you individually are loved, cared for, and respected. Use this lesson to enhance your life. My concern is that you do not fully appreciate how great God's love is for you individually. As your realization of His love fills your minds, it is time to put these lessons into practice in your daily life. As you become more loving and more aware of God's love, you begin to forge a peaceful coexistence with your fellow humans and your world. I have faith in you to love yourself, all of mankind, and your world, without judgment, or reservation.

Mary, Mother of Jesus.

Bibliography

Beattie, Melody (1987). *Co-Dependent No More.* New York: Harper/Hazelden.

Beattie, Melody (1989). *Beyond Co-Dependency.* New York: Harper & Row.

Bradshaw, John. Videos tapes and books.

Carnegie, Dale (1964). *How to Win Friends and Influence People.* New York: Simon and Schuster.

Dyer, Wayne W. (1976). *Your Erroneous Zones.* New York: Funk & Wagnalls.

Dyer, Wayne W. (1978). *Pulling Your Own Strings.* New York: T.Y Crowell Co.

Epstein, Gerald, M.D. (1989). *Healing Visualizations: Creating Health Through Imagery.* New York: Bantam Books.

Holmes, Ernest (1948). *This Thing Called You.* New York: Dodd, Mead & Company.

Jampolsky, Gerald (1979). *Love Is Letting Go of Fear.* Millbrae, CA: Celestial Arts.

Kirkwood, Annie (1994). *Mary's Message to the World.* New York: Putnam and Sons.

Kirkwood, Annie (1995). *Mary's Message of Hope.* Nevada City, CA: Blue Dolphin Publishing, Inc.

Kirkwood, Byron (1992). *Survival Guide for the New Millennium.* Nevada City, CA: Blue Dolphin Publishing, Inc.

Kirkwood, Annie & Kirkwood, Byron (1994). *Messages to Our Family.* Nevada City, CA: Blue Dolphin Publishing.

Kirkwood, Annie & Kirkwood, Byron (1997). *Instructions for the Soul.* Nevada City, CA: Blue Dolphin Publishing, Inc.

Ponder, Catherine (1966). *The Prospering Power of Love.* Marina Del Rey, CA: Devorss & Company.

Ponder, Catherine (1967). *The Healing Secret of the Ages.* West Nyack, NY: Parker Pub. Co.

Robinson, Bryan E., Ph.D. & McCullers, Jamey, R.N. (1994). *How to Learn to Love Yourself* (Healograms Series 2) and *611 Ways to Boost Your Self-Esteem.* Deerfield Beach, FL: Health Communications.

Thomas, T. (1990). *Surviving with Serenity.* Deerfield Beach, FL: Health Communications.

Williamson, Marianne (1992). *Return to Love: Reflections on the Principles of "A Course in Miracles."* New York: HarperCollins.

Annie Kirkwood travels giving talks, workshops, and seminars. Urging Annie to "Live the message," the Blessed Mother has directed Annie to encourage people to do the same. Annie speaks from the heart about her experiences and personal dedication to spiritual growth and healing. Annie began receiving messages in her mind from Mary, Mother of Jesus, in 1987 and continues to receive messages from Mary and other spiritual guides.

CPSIA information can be obtained at www.ICGtesting.com
Printed in the USA
LVOW12s2001311014

411466LV00001B/95/P